2023
Planetary Calendar Day Planner

with Astrological Forecasts

Ralph & Lahni DeAmicis

Published Continuously
Since 1949
Calculated for Pacific 'Clock Time'

Planetary Calendar   Cuore Libre Publishing

The 2023 Planetary Calendar Day Planner
By Ralph & Lahni DeAmicis

Planetary Calendar, an Imprint of
Cuore Libre Publishing
Napa, California
www.PlanetaryCalendar.com

Copyright 2023 Ralph & Lahni DeAmicis
ISBN 978-1-931163-25-5 at Ingram
No part of this calendar may be reproduced in
any form without permission from the publisher.

Cover Photo: NASA & The Jet Propulsion Laboratory

The Planetary Calendar is calculated in Solar Fire using Pacific 'Clock Time', so it adapts to Daylight Savings Time. Adjustments for the other North American time zones are found at the bottom of the 'Month at a Glance' pages. The charts are calculated for Sacramento, the capitol of California. We use this region not only because it is the center of our universe, but because the North Bay is one the longest continuously occupied regions in North America, so it clearly has good Feng Shui!

Disclaimer: Even though we make every effort to get the correct information into the correct places, there are thousands of data points, so errors occur. Also, we make every effort to provide trustworthy forecasts, based on generally accepted Astrological principles, but forecasting is, by its nature, subject to undetected influences that may skew the results. Therefore, we accept no responsibility for any losses or inconveniences you may suffer from using this information, although we truly hope you find it helpful.

Contents

Signs of the Zodiac - 4

Chapter 1: Welcome & Planning Ahead for 2023 - 5

Chapter 2: Using the Calendar - 7

Chapter 3: Reading the Calendar Layout - 9

Chapter 4: Text Ephemeris, Planetary Speed, Void of Course - 11

Chapter 5: About the Signs - 13

Chapter 6: About the Planets - 15

Chapter 7: About the Aspects - 17

Chapter 8: About the Calendar's Astrology - 19

The Monthly Charts, Forecasts, Month & Week at a Glance

January - 21	July - 111
February - 37	August - 125
March - 51	September - 139
April - 67	October - 153
May - 81	November - 169
June - 95	December - 183

Here's a Peek at 2024 - 198

Chapter 9: Healing with the Terra Map & Feng Shui Tips - 199

Ephemeris Grids - 205

About the Authors & Catalog - 217

Quick Reference Page - Timing with the Planets - 218

Quick Reference Pages - Retrogrades, Eclipses & Gardening - 219

Order Form for the 2024 Planetary Calendar - 220

The Signs of the Zodiac

Birth Date	Sign	Element	Quality	Ruling Planet
March 21 to April 19	Aries ♈	Fire	Cardinal	Mars ♂
April 20 to May 20	Taurus ♉	Earth	Fixed	Venus ♀
May 21 to June 20	Gemini ♊	Air	Mutable	Mercury ☿
June 21 to July 22	Cancer ♋	Water	Cardinal	Moon ☽
July 23 to August 22	Leo ♌	Fire	Fixed	Sun ☉
August 23 to Sept 22	Virgo ♍	Earth	Mutable	Mercury ☿
Sept 23 to Oct 22	Libra ♎	Air	Cardinal	Venus ♀
Oct 23 to Nov 21	Scorpio ♏	Water	Fixed	Tr. Mars ♂ Modern Ruler - Pluto ♇
Nov 22 to Dec 21	Sagittarius ♐	Fire	Mutable	Jupiter ♃
Dec 22 to Jan 19	Capricorn ♑	Earth	Cardinal	Saturn ♄
Jan 20 to Feb 18	Aquarius ♒	Air	Fixed	Tr. Saturn ♄ Modern Ruler - Uranus ♅
Feb 19 to March 20	Pisces ♓	Water	Mutable	Tr. Jupiter ♃ Modern Ruler - Neptune ♆

Traditional Ruling Signs from the Table of Dignities (pg. 15) are Signs where the Planet is most socially expressive in a Dynamic or Responsive manner. Note the Exaltation for the Sun is Aries and for the Moon is Taurus. Refer to page 8 for their daily application for Leos and Cancerians in place of the Sun and Moon.

Calendar Times are based on the Clock for Pacific Time, adjusting with Daylight Savings Time.

One: Welcome to The Planetary Calendar

From its start in 1949, this was intended as a teaching tool. Over the years, advanced information and features were added until it has become America's most sophisticated Astrological Calendar. At the same time other features were added so that students could easily use this information to benefit their lives. That trend continues this year as less helpful sections were removed in favor of expanded and clearer instructions. After seventy-three editions the Planetary Calendar continues to be a living document and we thank you for being part of this community.

New Features: We expanded the annotated Forecasts and included personalization for the Signs. The Day Blocks include the Degrees of the Full and New Moons. The instructions have been improved. There are quick reference pages at the back for using the Aspects daily for timing activities. The Ingress and Lunation Charts are now only found in the Day Planner and Electronic Calendar. To receive monthly forecast reminders email sales@spaceandtime.com and watch our videos at www.PlanetaryCalendar.com.

Planning for the Year Ahead: First, avoid planning important events during the Eclipse periods. They can be tumultuous and potentially life changing if you have major Planets or Angles near those Degrees. There is a New Moon Eclipse at 29 Degrees Aries on April 19th followed by the Full Moon Eclipse at 14 Degrees Taurus/Scorpio on May 5th, which overlaps a Mercury in Taurus Retrograde. Next, "The Great American New Moon Eclipse" at 21 Degrees Libra on Oct. 14th is followed by the Full Moon Eclipse at 5 Degrees Scorpio/Taurus on Oct. 28th. We suggest you watch our forecast video around that time.

Next, be aware of the Mercury Retrogrades since those times tend to be fraught with communication issues, so we suggest not making important purchases then if possible. The year begins and ends with Mercury Retrograde, which mostly happen in Earth Signs this year. Refer to page 219 for the Retrograde and Eclipse dates.

Here is how the year will likely unfold. While January will start off slowly, once we pass the Lunar New Year, all the planets have turned Direct so progress in the outer world will come more easily. When we combine that with a fast Jupiter and an accelerating Mars, expect the pace to pick up through May. But then through the Spring, Saturn enters Pisces, Pluto enters Aquarius and Jupiter joins Uranus in Taurus, so the year's theme will dramatically change when the alliances shift.

While Jupiter Sextile Saturn is good for the economy, Jupiter Square Pluto could signal emerging chaos in global affairs. By late Spring, environmental issues will come to the fore, an issue that will repeat in September.

By July, enough outer Planets are turning Retrograde that we should expect the economy to slow and take a breath. By the end of the Summer things may feel downright stalled as people focus on their relationships and personal wellbeing. In September, as Jupiter and Uranus get cozy in Taurus, there could be dramatic economic and climatic changes affecting the food supplies. Expect big court cases to be in the news as well as important new technologies emerging.

By the middle of Autumn, the outer planets are Retrograde while the inner planets are sending a muddled message. But by mid-October the Martial Scorpio energy will suddenly get more focused and determined so that Eclipse will be powerful, and it may take until December before the ripples from that settle.

Wishing you *Good Stars* in the Year Ahead

Ralph & Lahni DeAmicis

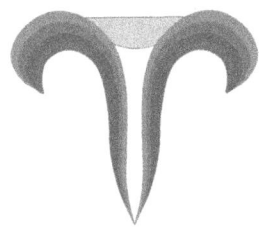

Two: Using the Calendar

Start by looking at the whole Day Block and divide it into four quadrants. When there are more Planetary Glyphs above the Date Number (Lunar Aspects) it indicates an easier social day. More Glyphs below make for a challenging day. More Glyphs above the Dotted Line (Planetary Aspects) indicate helpful connections in the outer world. Aspects below indicate challenges.

A Gray Frame on a Day Block denotes the
New Moon, Full Moon & the Sun's Ingress

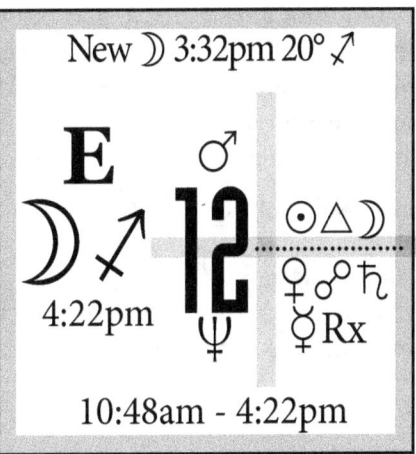

To the Right of the Line are the Sun and Planet Aspects

To the Left of the Line are the Signs of the Moon and its Aspects

Glyphs Above the Line are Supportive Aspects

Glyphs Below the Line are Challenging Aspects

A Void of Course Moon Time
ends when it enters the Next Sign

These four quadrants are easy to remember because they reflect the design of the human body. The upper body optimistically focuses on the future while the lower deals with the results. Your head thinks, 'Let's go for a walk', but it's your feet that are sore later! The left side of the body is the Lunar, emotional side, while the right is the Solar, more social side. The left is where you hold a baby's head, so they hear your heartbeat, but it's your right hand that you extend in greeting.

The 'upper' supportive Aspects are the Conjunction (0 degrees), Sextile (60 degrees) and Trine (120 degrees). The 'lower' or challenging Aspects are the Square (90 degrees) and the Opposition (180 degrees). When a day has mostly supportive Aspects, we mark it with a White Circle. When the challenging Aspects dominate, we put a Black Box around the Date. A Gray Frame found on a Day Block denotes the New Moon, Full Moon and the Sun's entrance (Ingress) into the next Sign. You can read about the Aspects to better understand their diverse influences on page 17.

Find your Sun Sign, Ruling Planet, and its Glyph on pages 4 & 14 to personalize your experience of the Calendar. When your Glyph appears above the Date, the day will feel easier as the Moon supports your talents. When it is below, you have to work harder to make things come out right. **Note: Cancer and Leo Sun Positions.** The Sun and Moon do not appear above and below the Date, so the Cancerians instead use Venus, the Ruler of feminine Taurus, the Sign of the Moon's Exaltation. The Leos use Mars, the Ruler of masculine Aries, the Sign of the Sun's Exaltation. The way we describe the Exalted position is as the 'Best Friend' or "Colleague".

When your Planetary Ruler appears above or below the Dotted Line, that Planet is making a significant connection with another Planet, indicating important things are happening in your life. While Aspects above the Line are supportive and below are challenging, the nature of the Planets and the Aspect that connects them will shape how it affects you. Planetary Aspects are felt for extended periods and the slower the Planet, the longer the duration of those effects. For example, Mercury to Venus Aspects may last a few days, while Saturn to Neptune Aspects can last weeks or longer. Read the pages about the Planets and the Aspects for a greater understanding of those differences.

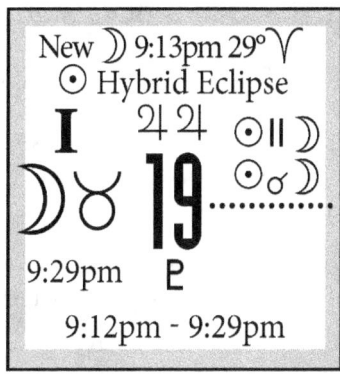

Three: Reading the Calendar Layout

The Upper Page

On either side of the Month and Year you will see the Signs that begin and end each month. Below that is the Forecast with the Capital Footnote (A) referencing the Dates on the Grid. The Forecast provides insights into the Planetary Transits, Direction changes (Retrograde or Direct) and Aspects. At the bottom of the page is the Glyph to English Key with Keywords to make understanding the calendar easier. See the expanded descriptions of the Signs, Planets and Aspects on pages 13 to 18.

The Lower Page

The Compact Text Ephemeris shows the Planetary Positions by Sign and Degree on the first day of the month, in plain language. It also shows any Planetary Sign changes and direction changes (Retrograde or Direct). There is a classic Table Ephemeris for the year after December, but the Compact Ephemeris is a quick reference for Planetary positions. At the bottom margin are calculations for four continental USA Time Zones. The Calendar is calculated for Pacific 'Clock' Time. There is no need to adjust your calculation for Daylight Savings Time unless your State does not use it.

What the Day Blocks Signify

Use the Date in the center as your reference

1) To the left is the symbol for the Moon and its current Sign.
2) Below that is the time when the Moon enters that Sign.
3) Above that is a letter that footnotes to the forecast. e.g '**A**'.
4) Above are the supportive Aspects (Conjunction, Sextile, Trine).
5) Below are the challenging Aspects (Square, Opposition).
The Lunar Aspects Above & Below the Date run
 from left to right, as they occur from early to late.
6) At the lower edge of the Box are the times of the Moon's Void
of Course (VOC) see pg. 31, which can span multiple days.
7) At the top edge of each box are the Planetary Ingresses,
Lunations, Eclipses, Meteors and Holidays.
8) To the right of the Date on the Dotted Line are the Planetary
Aspects. Supportive Aspects are above and Challenging Aspects are
below. Their time sequence runs from the Dotted Line up or Dotted
Line down, with the earliest Aspects touching the Line.

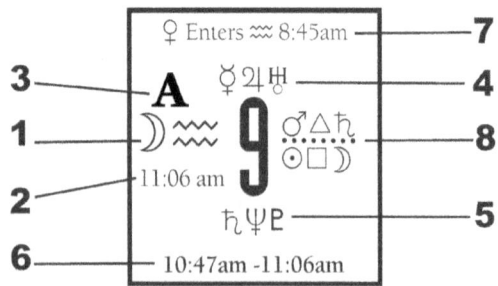

The only Lunar Aspects shown on the line are to the Sun. The Planetary Direction changes are also shown on the Dotted Line, 'D' for Direct is above the line and 'Rx' for Retrograde is below.

The **White Circle** denotes a day with mostly supportive Aspects, when new projects encounter minimum resistance. The **Black Box** around the Date denotes a day with challenging Aspects when new projects may require extra work. A **Gray Frame** denotes the Sun entering a Sign and the New or Full Moon

Four: Text Ephemeris, Planetary Speed & VOC

Mercury ☿ 10° Capricorn ♑ enters Aquarius ♒ on the 13th at 9:51am. Venus ♀ Rx 20° Capricorn ♑. Mars ♂ 21° Scorpio ♏ enters Sagittarius ♐ on the 13th at 1:52am. Jupiter ♃ 25° Aquarius ♒ enters Pisces ♓ on the 28th at 8:09pm. Saturn ♄ 8° Aquarius ♒. Uranus ♅ Rx 11° Taurus ♉. Neptune ♆ Rx 20° Pisces ♓. Pluto ♇ 25° Capricorn ♑.

The Text Ephemeris is easy to read because everything is in English and paired with the Astrology Glyphs. There is a full Ephemeris after December for long range planning. The Text Ephemeris shows the month's Planetary Movements, Sign and Direction changes, with degrees. The Solar and Lunar changes are shown in the Day Blocks. The Sun entering a new Sign and the New Moon and Full Moon are highlighted with a Gray Frame.

Start projects between the New and Full Moon because energy is rising. The Sun Trine Moon AVY after the Full Moon (Waning Gibbous) is when the energy is flowing most smoothly so that's a good time to overcome resistance. As Planets prepare to change Direction they slow from our perspective and issues related to them in our world will be harder to move forward.

When the Planets are moving fast, you have the wind at your back. Everything related to them happens more quickly and easily. That is why it is important to understand what each Planet signifies. In our Forecasts, we also take into account the speed of the Planets as indicators.

Some Planets change Sign and Direction more often. Here is a quick guide to each Planet's orbit.

Mercury: 88 days
Venus: 224.7 days
Earth: 365.256 days
Mars: 687 days
Jupiter: 11.86 years
Saturn: 29.5 years
Uranus: 84 years
Neptune: 164.8 years
Pluto: 248 years

While the inner Planets affect our daily lives, outer Planets affect our social standing. For example, Jupiter Returns to your birth position at ages 12, 24, 36, etc., often lucky years. Saturn takes 29.5-years to 'Return', once the average lifespan, thus Saturn's connection to maturity. The current lifespan is 78 years, closer to the orbit of Uranus, although with its 84-year orbit, many people never experience their Uranus Return. Our experience of Uranus, Neptune and Pluto, with their long orbits, is less personal and more gradual, often intangible. We imagine them like our utilities; they exist in the background and we don't notice them until the power, water or internet go out.

About the Void of Course (VOC) Moon

The period after the Moon's last Aspect to any Planet, until it enters the next Sign, is the Void of Course. Imagine the Moon as someone running between meetings who finds themselves at loose ends until the next. While this time may be potentially unproductive, it can also be a very creative time because it lacks an agenda. Also, some VOC periods are better than others. When the Moon is in Signs Ruled by Jupiter (Sagittarius & Pisces) or its own Rulership & Exaltation, (Cancer & Taurus) she is self-directed and resourceful so that time is less challenging.

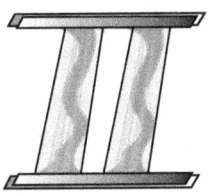

Five: About the Signs

To use the Calendar effectively you will need to know your Sun Sign and its Ruling Planet. It's important to understand what the Twelve Signs represent beyond the annual sequence of nature's seasons.

Planets are defined in four ways and each is a unique combination of those definitions: Polarity, Element, Quality and Planetary Ruler. The two Polarities are Masculine and Feminine. We can also call them Dynamic and Responsive.

Then there are the Four Elements: Fire, Earth, Air and Water. These represent the four States of Matter in physics: Plasma, Solid, Gaseous and Liquid. Masculine Fire energizes, Feminine Earth stabilizes, Masculine Air interacts and Feminine Water dissolves.

The Three Qualities represent the stages within the annual cycle of the seasons: Cardinal initiates, Fixed systemizes and Mutable humanizes.

The Planets are related to the Signs in complex ways described by the Table of Planetary Dignities. Each Planet has six Signs that it relates to most directly, but in the Calendar we want you to use what is called the Planet's 'Ruling' Signs, the most socially active Dynamic and Responsive positions.

We use the classic, traditional Rulers, so there are no Rulerships assigned to Uranus, Neptune or Pluto. If you learned Astrology in the fifties, sixties and seventies, this may seem bizarre but the Astrologers who assigned the 'modern' Rulers had limited understanding of the underlying Geometry at work. They also had almost no data on the newly discovered Planets to base those decisions. That mean both **Aries** and **Scorpio** will look for **Mars** above or below the Date and Dotted Line in the Day Blocks as an indicator about the day. **Sagittarius** and **Pisces** will look for **Jupiter**. **Capricorn** and **Aquarius** will look for **Saturn**.

The Twelve Signs
Planetary Ruler, Quality, Element, Action, Opposite Sign

♈ **Aries**: ♂ Mars, Cardinal, Fire, Initiates, ♎
The symbol is the Ram. They are energetic.
♉ **Taurus**: ♀ Venus, Fixed, Earth, Stabilizes, ♏
The symbol is the Bull. They are patient.
♊ **Gemini**: ☿ Mercury, Mutable, Air, Interacts, ♐
The symbol is the Twins are in arm. They are engaging.
♋ **Cancer**: ♂ Moon, Cardinal, Water, Nurtures, ♑
The symbol is the Crabs. They are protective.
♌ **Leo**: ☉ Sun, Fixed, Fire, Creates, ♒
The symbol is the Lion. They are dramatic.
♍ **Virgo**: ☿ Mercury, Mutable, Earth, Perfect, ♓
The symbol is the Virgin. They are diligent.
♎ **Libra**: ♀ Venus, Cardinal, Air, Balances, ♈
The symbol is the Scales. They are considerate.
♏ **Scorpio**: ♂ Mars, Fixed, Water, Manages, ♉
The symbol is the Scorpion. They are daring.
♐ **Sagittarius**: ♃ Jupiter, Mutable, Fire, Optimizes, ♊
The symbol is the Centaur's bow & arrow. They are confident.
♑ **Capricorn**: ♄ Saturn, Cardinal, Earth, Codifies, ♋
The symbol is the Sea Goat. They are dependable.
♒ **Aquarius**: ♄ Saturn, Fixed, Air, Innovates, ♌
The symbol is the Water Bearer. They are revolutionary.
♓ **Pisces**: ♃ Jupiter, Mutable, Water, Unites, ♍
The symbol is the Fishes. They are philosophical.

The Amicis Table of Dignities						
Celestial Body	Dynamic Ruler	Responsive Ruler	Exalted Sign	Dynamic Detriment	Responsive Detriment	Fall Sign
☉	♌	♋ v	♈	♒	♑ v	♎
☾	♐ v	♋	♉	♊ v	♑	♏
☿	♊	♍	♒	♐	♓	♌
♀	♎	♉	♓	♈	♏	♍
♂	♈	♏	♑	♎	♉	♋
♃	♐	♓	♋	♊	♍	♑
♄	♑	♒	♎	♋	♌	♈
⚳	♊	♍	♏	♐	♓	♉

Dotted Line Designates a Primary Sign & V a Vice Sign. www.SpaceAndTime.com (C) 2018 R & L De Amicis

Six: About the Planets

The Calendar shows the every changing dynamics between the Planets and how they influence us through these Aspects. Our descriptions of the Planets are about the nature of the energy that they bring to those meetings. To understand the Planets you need to see them in their various guises and that is what our Table of Dignities reveals. In the same way that we act differently at work or home, with friends or family, the Planets each have six roles they play on the Astrological stage. They have three Social roles: the two Rulers and the Exaltation, and three Personal roles: the two Detriments and the Fall.

To learn more, read the Calendar's Companion Book for a non-misogynistic explanation of this vital interpretation tool. To that end, we have replaced Masculine and Feminine with Dynamic and Resposive. When Planets are in Aspect, the 'current' is flowing. If you jump into projects when the Aspects are Supportive, you can ride the tides. If you start when they are Challenging, you'll be bucking the flow.

How Planets Act When they Make a Connection

When the **Sun** ☉ makes an Aspect, it brings energy to that Planet. When Supportive, it promotes stability. When Challenged, it bullies. The Sun's Dynamic Ruling Sign is Leo; Cancer is its Receptive Ruler and Aries is its Exaltation. In those Signs, the Sun lives for the outer, social world. In the opposite Signs, Aquarius, Capricorn and Libra, the Sun is concerned for the personal life.

When the **Moon** ☽ makes an Aspect, it lends emotional oomph to the relationship. Supportive; it's a helping hand. Challenged; it's a slap. The Social Trilogy is Cancer, Sagittarius and Taurus.
The Personal Trilogy is Capricorn, Gemini and Scorpio.

When **Mercury** ☿ connects it promotes engagement. Supportive; it provides good information. Challenged; it teases and tests.
When **Venus** ♀ connects, beauty and indulgence arrive. Supportive; it's graceful and artistic. Challenged; it is indulgent.
When **Mars** ♂ connects passions heat up. Supportive; it is protective, engaging. Challenged; defensive, destructive.
When **Jupiter** ♃ connects horizons, possibilities & imagination expand. Supportive; it rescues. Challenged; it runs roughshod.
When **Saturn** ♄ connects it provides maturity, discipline, structure. Supportive; a protective wall. Challenged; a limiting fence.
When **Uranus** ♅ connects it electrifies, networks & communicates. Supportive; it is a community. Challenged; it is a gang.
When **Neptune** ♆ connects it expands us beyond the visible. Supportive; new levels of perception. Challenged; confusion.
When **Pluto** ♇ connects it amplifies, intensifies. Supportive; strong gets stronger. Challenged; magnifies the weaknesses.

Seven: About the Aspects

Aspects are the angles made between the Sun, Moon, Planets, Ascendant and Midheaven. As an Astrological tool, it's like a family tree crossed with a wiring diagram. While individual Planets show a person's talents, the Aspects show the Planets either working in concert (Conjunct 0°), being mutually supportive (Sextile 60° & Trine 120°), or being demanding (Square 90° & Opposition 180°). A less used Aspect is the Parallel, that shows when Planets have a similar status.

☌ **Conjunction** - 0 to 7 Degrees - The Planets are close together, deciding and working in concert.

✳ **Sextile** - 60 Degrees - Because they live nearby and share a Polarity, the Sextile creates an easy, supportive relationship, like cousins working and playing together.

□ **Square** - 90 Degrees - Imagine cars meeting at an intersection. The drivers must use the rules and their wits to get where they're going and avoid crashing.

△ **Trine** - 120 Degrees - This harmonious, strongly supportive connection is like siblings who provide the muscle and resources each other needs without question.

☍ **Opposition** - 180 Degrees - Imagine two people sitting opposite each other negotiating. While each is committed to their position, they need something from each other.

∥ **Parallel** - 0 degrees of Latitude - This notes Planets equally North or South of the Ecliptic, holding equal status, or rank. By itself it's not significant, but it eases the way for any other Aspect. The related Aspect, the Contra Parallel, which is marked by the parallel lines with an angled line crossing them, represents Planets at opposite distances above and below the Ecliptic. This describes a mentor relationship in which the lower Planet is the beneficiary of the upper. We don't list the Contra Parallel, although we consider it in our forecasts.

When looking at the Aspects, consider what each Planet does for the other. The ☉ Sun energizes, the ☽ Moon comforts,
☿ Mercury engages, ♀ Venus charms, ♂ Mars confronts,
♃ Jupiter expands, ♄ Saturn compresses, ♅ Uranus disrupts,
♆ Neptune envisions and ♇ Pluto empowers.

The Aspects determine how they contribute. The ☌ Conjunction unifies. The ✶ Sextile and △ Trine help without causing trouble. The □ Square and ☍ Opposition build and noisily bang into each other, because that's the nature of work.

The Aspects involving the Sun, Moon, Mercury, Venus, Mars and the Ascendant are felt personally. Those involving Jupiter, Saturn and the Midheaven are experienced socially. Aspects involving Uranus, Neptune and Pluto are felt gradually, because they change Signs so slowly, maintaining Aspects for long periods.

Outer planet Aspects are like sitting on a boat deck with friends and a big bottle of wine, enjoying the afternoon turning into evening. As the tide rolls in and the boat gradually rises, no one notices. It's only later, as they step down to the dock, that they'll recognize the change. Outer Planet Aspects are a different experience from the inner Planetary Aspects that say, *'Bam! Wake Up, Mars is Here!'*

Eight: About the Calendar's Astrology

The calendar's Astrology has three parts: Planets that act, Signs that are the actions, and the Aspects between the Planets. An Astrology Chart is a cosmic weather report based on the laws of physics and observation. The ephemeris shows the Planetary positions in the future, so we can look for when those patterns appeared in the past for clues about possible upcoming events. In comparison, Astrology Calendars look at the ongoing Planetary movements and the relationships they form and dissolve over time. We make a big deal when slow-moving Planets change Sign, because that means that economic or social movements will be changing.

The information in the Day Blocks include the major Planets and the traditional Aspects: Conjunctions, Sextiles, Squares, Trines, Oppositions, plus Parallels. In the written forecasts we add the major Asteroids and Chiron and rely on our own Table of Dignities, to show how the Planets perform in diverse Signs. We prefer that to the highly misogynistic table that came to us from Medieval times. Our table is based on Sacred Geometry and it includes dual Rulers for the Sun and the Moon, a concept that was always in the Astrology of Ancient Greece. You can read more about that in the Calendar's companion book. To prepare the calendar, we generate data reports of the major Aspects, charts for all the Solar Ingresses and Lunations and Astro*Carto*Graphy maps using the current Solar Fire Software.

The written monthly forecasts and year ahead preview are our personal interpretations of what we see in the Charts. The Letters (Footnotes) that connect the Day Blocks to the Forecast highlight significant Astrological events. On the Planetary Calendar website, we post video forecasts to supplement these written ones. The Signs that we mention in the comments can apply to your Sun position, but equally to your Moon or Ascendant.

"As the Sun Rules the Day, the Moon Rules the Night", so you may find that your Moon is the stronger 'Light' in your Chart. You may resonate more personally with Aspects involving your Moon Sign and its Ruler. The secret is to know your own Chart well. That way you will recognize when the messages are for you. We hope you find it helpful and illuminating.

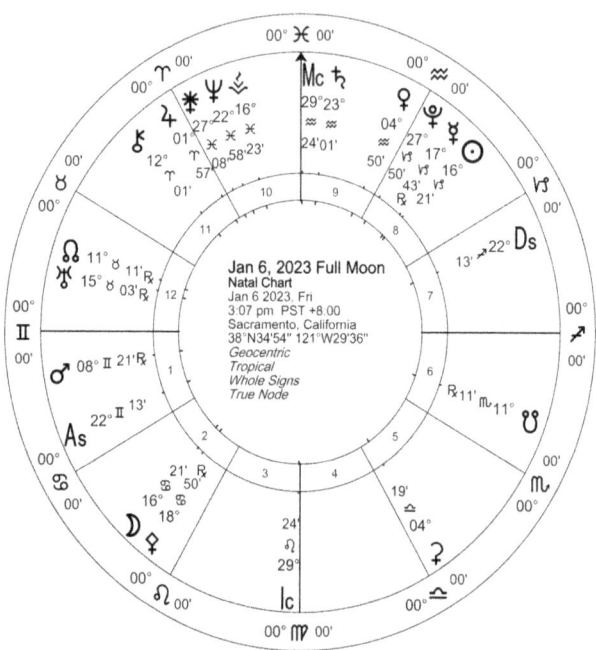

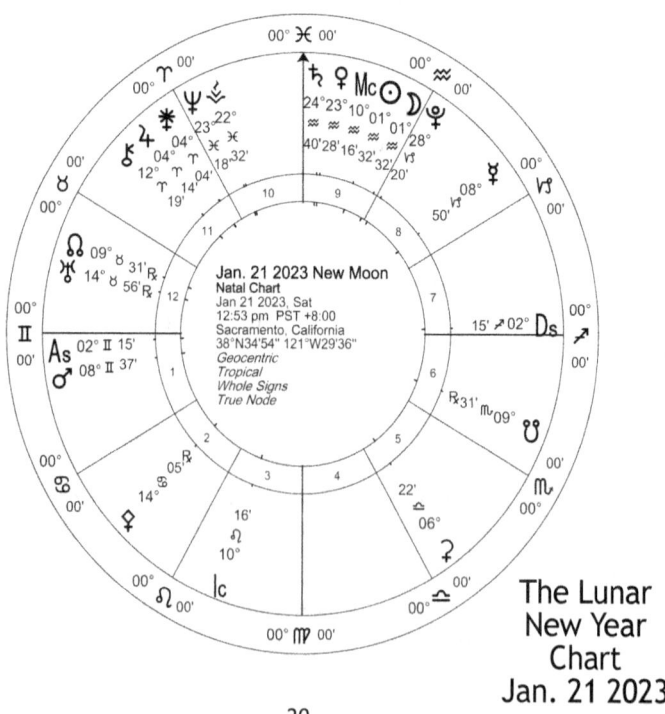

The Lunar New Year Chart Jan. 21 2023

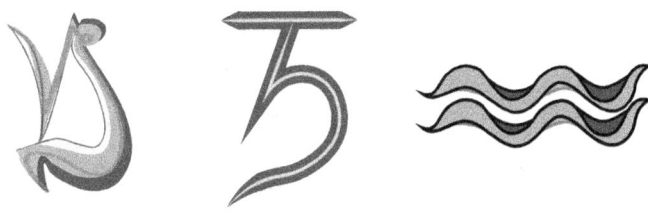

January Forecasts
With Annotated Footnotes (A)
♑ **Capricorn the Sea Goat to** ♒ **Aquarius the Water Pourer**

This year the start of our Gregorian Calendar and that of the Asian Lunar Calendar or Chinese New Year (CNY) are almost in sync because the New Moon in Aquarius that marks the CNY is so early on January 21st, beginning the Year of the Water Rabbit. Watch our CNY forecast at PlanetaryCalendar.com starting in December for our in depth look ahead at the coming year.

(A) The year starts with an exciting White Circle Day as Uranus both Conjuncts and Parallels the Moon, which is Trine the Sun, while Mercury Sextiles Neptune. A great day for reaching out to others through the phone, and electronically. As the Month progresses and Planets turn Direct, things get easier. Lean on the Earth Signs, Taurus, Virgo and Capricorn in your chart.

(B) Watch out for over stimulation as Venus enters hyper social Aquarius and the Moon contacts six planets as shown by the glyphs above and below the number. Aquarius, prepare to feel charming and attractive.

(C) At the Capricorn/Cancer Full Moon, the Cardinal Signs, Aries, Cancer, Libra and Capricorn, should hold onto something and pay attention because potentially disruptive forces are at work.

(D) The Sun Conjunct Mercury can burn out mental circuits in the days around this event so don't overload your brain. Both Capricorn and Cancer should beware!

(E) Physical frustration eases as Mars in Gemini turns Direct, making life easier for the Air Signs, Gemini, Libra and Aquarius.

(F) Plan to have something practical to do today and think outside the stylistic box. We're talking to you Libra!

(G) This is a nicely social day when you can have significant conversations about work and business strategies.

(H) Mercury turns Direct in practical Capricorn easing the mental
frustration while the Sun Conjuncts Pluto, so plan some alone time.

(I) The Sun enters Aquarius so let more light into your life. Literally, open the curtains to boost your mood!

(J) The New Moon marking the Lunar New Year is very early this year, heralding an early Spring, well before the Groundhog notices. However, this is the low ebb of the year when the energy of the Earth is most
withdrawn and unavailable for us so conserve your strength.

(K) Uranus turns Direct as Venus Conjuncts Saturn so change some outdated traditions, Taurus, Leo, Scorpio and Aquarius.

(L) The White Circle makes a social day when optimism is the rule, especially for Capricorn and Pisces.

(M) Venus enters Pisces, a compassionate and dreamy position and good for the Water Signs, Cancer, Scorpio and Pisces. Find ways to connect with your wider community for spiritual enrichment.

(N) Another pair of Circles heralds a time when positive changes in diet and exercise get a boost. Do the research and make the changes.

(O) With Jupiter and Mars supporting the Moon while the Sun Trines the Moon, whatever you choose to do, you will have the wind at your back.

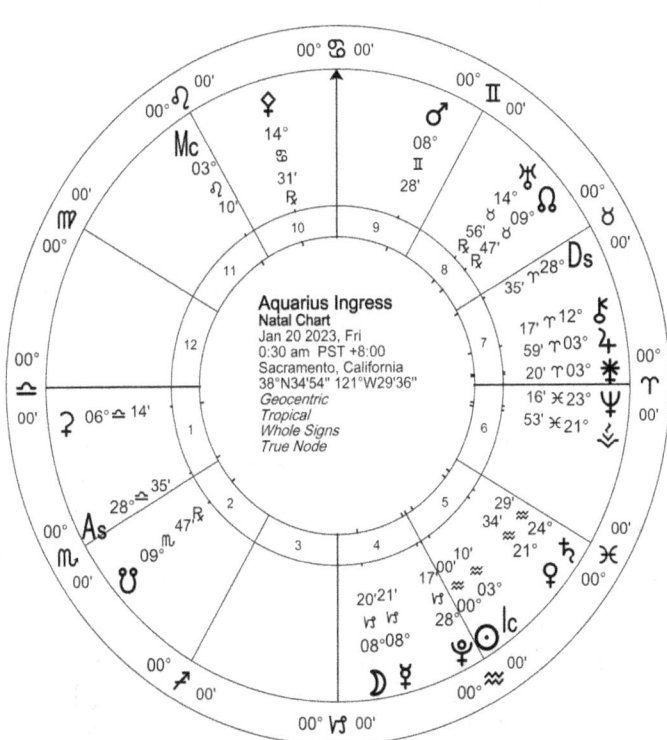

Signs

♈ Aries Begins
♉ Taurus Owns
♊ Gemini Engages
♋ Cancer Nurtures
♌ Leo Embraces
♍ Virgo Improves
♎ Libra Commits
♏ Scorpio Manages
♐ Sagittarius Views
♑ Capricorn Climbs
♒ Aquarius Herds
♓ Pisces Dreams

Planets

☉ Sun Spirit
☽ Moon Emotes
☿ Mercury Thinks
♀ Venus Feels
♂ Mars Acts
♃ Jupiter Expands
♄ Saturn Contracts
♅ Uranus Disrupts
♆ Neptune Envisions
♇ Pluto Unearths

Aspects

☌ Conjunct 0° Aligns
∥ Parallel 0° Equals
✶ Sextile 60° Helps
□ Square 90° Works
△ Trine 120° Supports
☍ Opposition 180° Counters

Ambitious Capricorn says "I Achieve"

Astro Notes:

JANUARY 2023

Sunday	Monday	Tuesday
New Year's Day — A — 1	♀ Enters ♒ 6:09pm — B — 2 — 6:43pm — 2:16pm - 6:43pm	Asarah B' Tevet Quadrantid Meteors — 3
8	9 — 5:52pm	10 — 7:15am — 7:15am
Martin Luther King — 15 — 4:08am — 12:39am - 4:08am	16	G — 17 — 9:32am — 6:26am - 9:32am
Lunar New Year — K — 22 — Year of the Water Rabbit	23 — 9:35am — 2:18am - 9:35am	L — 24
N — 29 — 9:51pm	O — 30 — 12:34am — 12:34am	31

All calculations are Pacific Clock Time (PST & PDT)

24

Mercury ☿ Rx 23° Capricorn ♑ turns Direct on the 18th at 5:11am at 8° ♑. Venus ♀ 27° Capricorn ♑ enters Aquarius ♒ on the 2nd at 6:09pm, enters Pisces ♓ on the 26th at 6:32pm. Mars ♂ Rx 9° Gemini ♊ turns Direct on the 12th at 12:56pm at 8° ♊. Jupiter ♃ 1° Aries ♈. Saturn ♄ 22° Aquarius ♒. Uranus ♅ Rx 15° Taurus ♉ turns Direct on the 22nd at 2:58pm at 14° ♉. Neptune ♆ 22° Pisces ♓. Pluto ♇ 27° Capricorn ♑.

January 2023

Wednesday	Thursday	Friday	Saturday
Quadrantid Meteors		Full ☽ 3:07pm 16° ♋	Orthodox Christmas Day
☽♊ 4 ♀⚹♃ ♄ ☽♋ 5 ☉△♅ C ☽♋ 6 ♅ ☿ ☉☍☽ D ☽♌ 7 ♆♃♂ ☉☌☿ ♇			
♆ 4:07pm	6:14am ♃ 6:14am	Epiphany - 3 King's Day	6:39pm 2:22pm - 6:39pm
			3rd Quarter ☽ 6:10pm
☿♅ ☽♍ 11	E ♇ ♂'D' ☽♎ 12 ☉△☽ 6:56pm ♆ 3:06pm - 6:56pm	♂♀♆ ☽♎ 13 ☉⚹♆ ♃ ☿	F ♄ ☽♎ 14 ♀□♅ ☉□☽
		☉ Enters ♒ 12:30am	New ☽ 12:53pm 01° ♒
H ☉∥☿ ♀ ☉☌♇ ☽♐ 18 ☿'D'	☽♑ 19 ♄ 11:11am ♆♃ 2:08am - 11:11am	I ☿♅ ☽♑ 20	J ♆♇♃ ☽♒ 21 ☉☌☽ 10:28am 7:52am - 10:28am
	♀ Enters ♓ 6:32pm		1st Quarter ☽ 7:18am
♆♃ ☽♈ 25 ☉⚹☽ 10:47am 8:11am - 10:47am	M ♃♂ ☽♈ 26 ☿	♄♀ ☽♉ 27 3:42pm ♇ 1:00pm - 3:42pm	♅☿♅ ☽♉ 28 ☉□☽

Add 1 Hour for Mountain Time (MT) - Add 2 Hours for Central Time (CT) - Add 3 Hours for Eastern Time (ET)

December 2022 to January 2023

Monday
Chanukah (Last Day)
Kwanzaa (1st Day)

☽ ♓ **26** ♄
11:33pm

10:19am - 11:33pm

Tuesday

☽ ♓ **27** ♀☋♇
☉⚹☽
♂

Wednesday

☽ ♓ **28** ♅♆♀♇
♀⚹♆
10:20pm

Thursday
1st Quarter ☽ 5:20pm

☽ ♈ **29** ♃♂
2:36am   ☿☌♀
          ☿ Rx
          ☉□☽

---------- 2:36am

December 26 thru January 1

Friday

☽ ♈ **30** ♄
       ☿

Saturday
New Year's Eve

☽ ♉ **31** ♀ ☌ ♇
9:08am   ♀ ♇

4:43am - 9:08am

Sunday
New Year's Day

A ⛢ ☿ ✶ ♆
☽ ♉ **1** ☉ △ ☽

January 2023

Monday
♀ Enters ♒ 6:09pm

B ☿ΨPM♀♃
☽♊ 2
6:43pm ♄

2:16pm - 6:43pm

Tuesday
Asarah B' Tevet
Quadrantid Meteors

♂♂
☽♊ 3 ☉♊P

Wednesday
Quadrantid Meteors

♄
☽♊ 4 ♀✶♃
Ψ

4:07pm

Thursday

☽♋ 5 ☉△♅
6:14am ♃

6:14am

28

January 2 thru 8

Friday

Full ☽ 3:07pm 16° ♋

C ☊
☽♋ **6** ☉☌☍☽
        ☿

Epiphany - 3 King's Day

Saturday

Orthodox Christmas Day

D ♆♃♂
☽♌ **7** ☉☌☿
6:39pm ♇

2:22pm - 6:39pm

Sunday

            ♂
☽♌ **8** ☿△♅
            ♀

29

January 2023

Monday

☽♌ **9** ☿∥♀ ♀△♂ ♅♄
5:52pm ---------

Tuesday

☽♍ **10** ♅ ♂
7:15am
--------- 7:15am

Wednesday

☽♍ **11** ☿♅

Thursday

E ♇ ♂'D'
☽♎ **12** ⊙△☽ ♆
6:56pm
3:06pm - 6:56pm

30

January 9 thru 15

Friday

☽♎ **13** ♂♀♆ ☉⚹♆ ♃☿

Saturday

3rd Quarter ☽ 6:10pm

F ☽♎ ♄ **14** ♀□♅ ☉□☽

Sunday

☽♏ **15** ☿♄
4:08am ♇
12:39am - 4:08am

January 2023

Monday
Martin Luther King

☽♏ 16 ♆
♅♀♄

Tuesday

G ☿ P P ♃ ☉ ⚹ ☽
☽♐ 17 ☉∥☽
9:32am ♂
6:26am - 9:32am

Wednesday

H ♀ ☉∥☿
☽♐ 18 ☉☌P
☿'D'

Thursday

☽♑ 19 ♄
11:11am ♆♃
2:08am -11:11am

January 16 thru 22

Friday
☉ Enters ♒ 12:30am

I ☿♅
☽♑ **20**

Saturday
New ☽ 12:53pm 01° ♒

J ♆♇♃
☽♒ **21** ☉☌☽

10:28am

7:52am - 10:28am

Sunday
Lunar New Year

K ♂♇☿ ☉♊☽ ♅'D'
☽♒ **22** ♀☌♄
♅

Year of the Water Rabbit

January 2023

Monday

☽♓ (**23** ♄♀♄♀ ♀∥♄
9:35am   ♂
2:18am - 9:35am

Tuesday

L   ☿♅♆
☽♓ (**24** ☉⚹♃

Wednesday

♆♇♃
☽♈ **25** ☉⚹☽
10:47am
8:11am - 10:47am

Thursday

♀ Enters ♓ 6:32pm

M   ♃♂
☽♈ **26**
     ☿

January 23 thru 29

Friday

☽ ♉ ♄♀ **27**
3:42pm P

1:00pm - 3:42pm

Saturday

1st Quarter ☽ 7:18am

☽ ♉ ♅☿♅ **28**
⊙□☽

Sunday

☽ ♉ ♆♇ ☿△♅ **29**
⊙△♂
♄
9:51pm

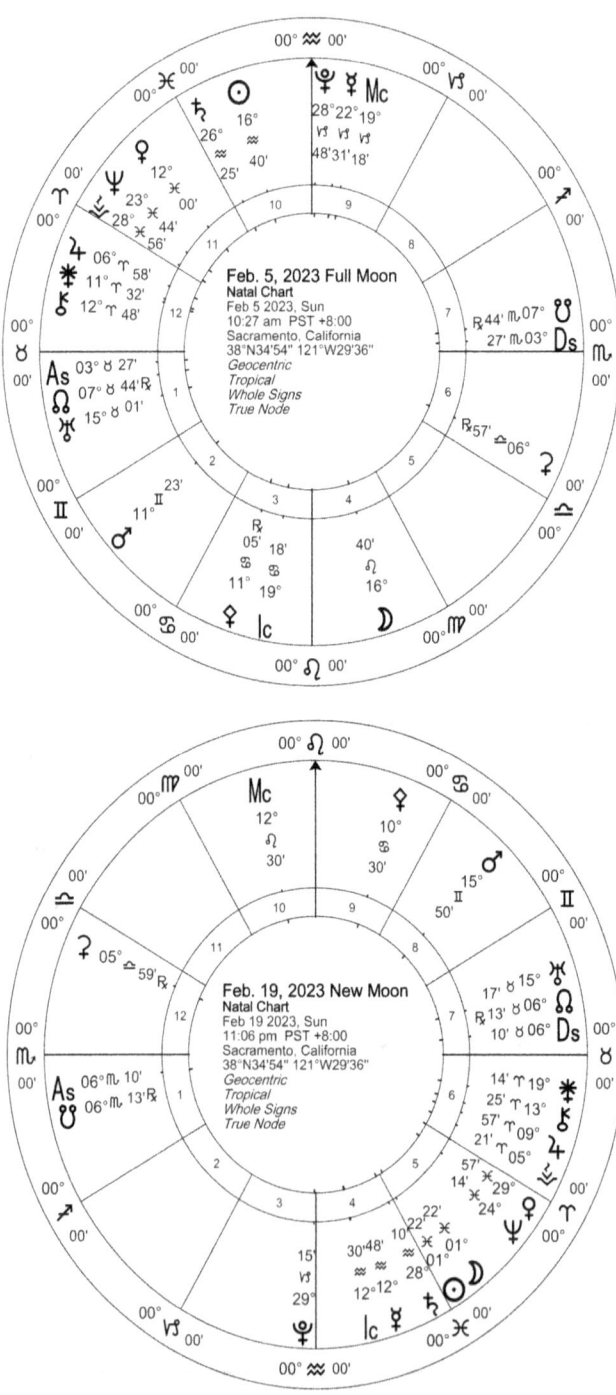

February Forecasts
With Annotated Footnotes (A)
≈ Aquarius the Water Pourer to ⟩(Pisces the Fishes

Note the simplicity of the ephemeris box this month. It's an indication that very few changes happen astrologically in February. Only Mercury and Venus change Signs and no Planets change direction. Mercury is speeding up after turning Direct in January, so communication is accelerating. All the Planets are Direct this month and that trend continues through March, so you can make great personal progress while events in the outer world also move along quickly. This trend reverses during the Summer when multiple outer Planets are Retrograde and world events may feel stalled. In March dramatic Sign changes are going to happen so enjoy the calm of February while you can.

(A) The Sun Square Uranus may shake the windows as stability encounters disruption, especially for Aquarius and Taurus.

(B) This disruptive trend will continue through the Full Moon, watch for where you have Leo and Aquarius in your chart because the Transits will energize those areas.

(C) The noise of last weekend will fade thanks to the Sun Trine Moon in Libra so it's an ideal time to seek cooperation and common ground with others. Mercury Conjunct Pluto suggests making private time for meditation. Very important for Gemini and Virgo.

(D) Mercury entering Aquarius adds brilliance to the mix, so focus on the area in your chart where you have that Sign. This is an excellent position for networking, social organization and technology projects. Good for the Air Signs Gemini, Libra and especially Aquarius.

(E) Venus Conjunct Neptune in Pisces opens the doors to compassion and imagination. Step through them if you want to increase your intuition and spiritual sensitivity. Pisces, take an herbal bath to calm your system.

(F) The Sun Conjunct Saturn is a big Aspect that will be active all week. Saturn suppresses the Solar Energy so expect this feeling to be pervasive in your community.

(G) The Sun enters Pisces, beginning the final thirty days of Winter when the debris of last year dissolves with the melting snow to feed the seeds of the coming Spring. On the 17th, Mercury Sextiled Jupiter so weekend errands and enterprise will go smoothly. Good for the Water Signs
Cancer, Scorpio and Pisces.

(H) The New Moon in Pisces is early in the Sign so it will feel like a low ebb, similar to the previous New Moon in Aquarius. But Venus entering Aries, well in advance of the Sun, adds a spark of fire to the mix. It could turn into a very interesting weekend when new passions and love interests arise. Aries gets a sparkle in their eyes.

(I) This is a wonderfully social day so take advantage of these lovely transits and get out and do something together.

(J) The Sun Sextile the Moon, that is also Conjunct Uranus, could kick off a very interesting weekend. Enjoy! Especially Good for Pisces and Taurus.

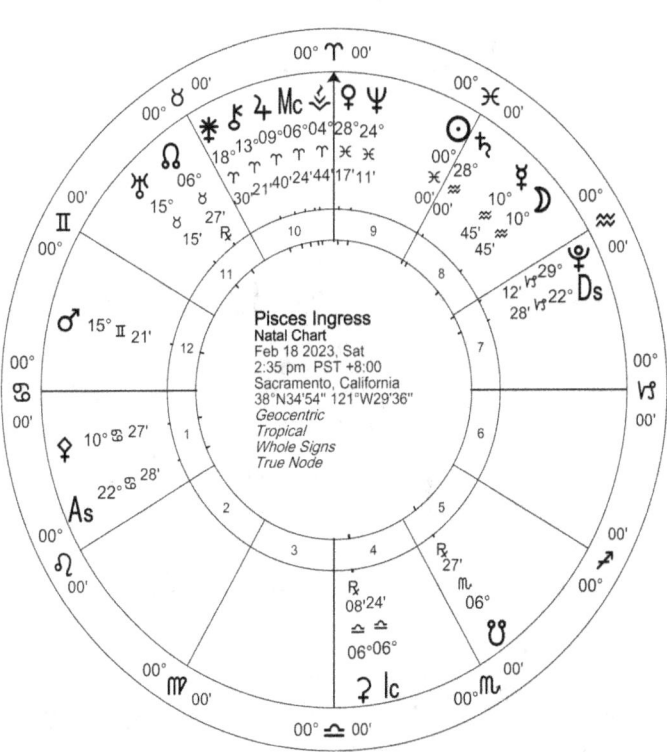

Signs

♈ Aries Begins
♉ Taurus Owns
♊ Gemini Engages
♋ Cancer Nurtures
♌ Leo Embraces
♍ Virgo Improves
♎ Libra Commits
♏ Scorpio Manages
♐ Sagittarius Views
♑ Capricorn Climbs
♒ Aquarius Herds
♓ Pisces Dreams

Planets

☉ Sun Spirit
☽ Moon Emotes
☿ Mercury Thinks
♀ Venus Feels
♂ Mars Acts
♃ Jupiter Expands
♄ Saturn Contracts
♅ Uranus Disrupts
♆ Neptune Envisions
♇ Pluto Unearths

Aspects

☌ Conjunct 0° Aligns
∥ Parallel 0° Equals
✶ Sextile 60° Helps
□ Square 90° Works
△ Trine 120° Supports
☍ Opposition 180° Counters

Innovative Aquarius says "I Network"

Astro Notes:

FEBRUARY 2023

Sunday	Monday	Tuesday
Full ☽ 10:27am 16° ♌ **B** ☽♌ **5** ☉♂☽ ♅	Tu B'Shevat ☽♍ **6** ☿✶♆ 1:13pm ♄ 6:15am - 1:13pm	☽♍ **7** ♀✶♅ ♂♀
Super Bowl ☽♏ **12** ☉∥♄ ♅	3rd Quarter ☽ 8:00am ♀♆☿♇ ☽♐ **13** ☉□☽ 5:30pm ♄ 3:51pm - 5:30pm	Valentine's Day ☿♃ ☽♐ **14** ♂
New ☽ 11:06pm 01°♓ ♀ Enters ♈ 11:55pm **H** ☿♄ ☉♂☽ ☽♓ **19** ♀✶♇ 8:55pm 6:00pm - 8:55pm	President's Day ♄♅ ☽♓ **20** ☉∥☽ ♂	Mardi Gras ♆♇ ☽♈ **21** 9:13pm ☿□♅ 8:05pm - 9:13pm
♇ ☽♊ **26** 7:47am ♄ 6:42am - 7:47am	1st Quarter ☽ 12:05am ♀♃♂♂ ☽♊ **27** ☉□☽	☿♄ ☽♋ **28** ♀∥♃ 6:39pm ♆ 5:07pm - 6:39pm

All calculations are Pacific Clock Time (PST & PDT)

Mercury ☿ 17° Capricorn ♑ enters Aquarius ♒ on the 11th at 3:22am. Venus ♀ 6° Pisces ♓ enters Aries ♈ on the 19th at 11:55pm. Mars ♂ 10° Gemini ♊. Jupiter ♃ 6° Aries ♈. Saturn ♄ 25° Aquarius ♒. Uranus ♅ 14° Taurus ♉. Neptune ♆ 23° Pisces ♓. Pluto ♇ 28° Capricorn ♑.

February 2023

Wednesday	Thursday	Friday	Saturday
☽♋ **1** ♄ 12:11pm 3:57am - 12:11pm	Groundhog Day ☽♋ **2** ♀♅ ♃	**A** ☽♋ **3** ♆ ☉□♅ ☿♇ 10:18pm --------	☽♌ **4** ♂♃♂ 12:48am ♀□♂ -------- 12:48am
☽♍ **8** ☿♇ ♆ 10:39pm --------	☽♎ **9** 12:46am ♃ -------- 12:46am	**C** ☽♎ **10** ♂♆♀ ☉△☽ ☿♂♇	☿ Enters ♒ 3:22am **D** ☽♏ **11** ♄♄ ☉∥☽ 10:34am ♇☿ 8:41am - 10:34am
E ☽♐ **15** ♄ ☉⚹☽ ♀∥♆ ☿♂♆ 8:59pm ♆♀ 5:05pm - 8:59pm	**F** ☽♐ **16** ♅ ☉♂♄ ♃	☽♒ **17** ♆♀♇ ☿⚹♃ 9:34pm 8:17pm - 9:34pm	☉ Enters ♓ 2:35pm **G** ☽♒ **18** ♃♇☿♂ ♅ Maha Shivaratri Isra and Mi'raj
Ash Wednesday **I** ☽♈ **22** ♀♀♃♃ ☿△♂	☽♈ **23** ♂☿♄ ♇ 11:21pm --------	**J** ☽♉ **24** ♅ ☉⚹☽ 12:28am -------- 12:28am	☽♉ **25** ♅♆ ☿

Add 1 Hour for Mountain Time (MT) - Add 2 Hours for Central Time (CT) - Add 3 Hours for Eastern Time (ET)

February 2023

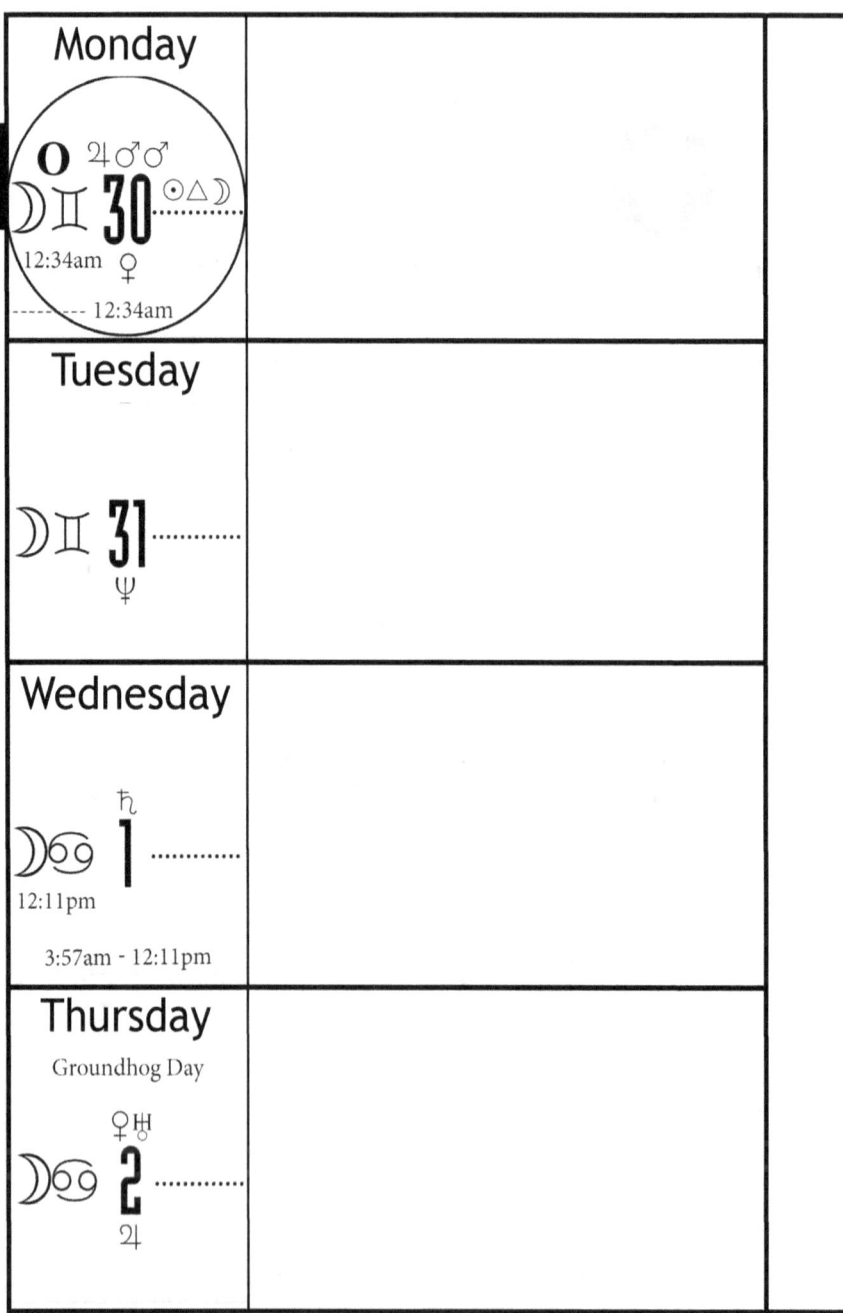

January 30 thru February 5

Friday

A

☽︎ ☌ ♋︎ **3** ♆
          ☉ □ ♅
☿ ♇

10:18pm

Saturday

          ♂ ♃ ☌
☽︎ ♌ **4**
12:48am   ♀ □ ♂

--------- 12:48am

Sunday

Full ☽︎ 10:27am 16° ♌︎

B

☽︎ ♌ **5**
              ☉ ☍ ☽︎
♅

43

February 2023

Monday
Tu B'Shevat

☽♍ 6 ⛢ ☿✶♆
1:13pm ♄
6:15am - 1:13pm

Tuesday

☽♍ 7 ⛢ ♀✶⛢
♂♀

Wednesday

☽♍ 8 ☿♇
♆
10:39pm

Thursday

☽♎ 9
12:46am ♃
-------- 12:46am

February 6 thru 12

Friday

C ♂♆♀ ☉△☽
☽♎ **10** ☿♂♇

Saturday

☿ Enters ♒ 3:22am

D ♄♄
☽♏ **11** ☉∥☽
10:34am ♇☿

8:41am - 10:34am

Sunday
Super Bowl

☽♏ **12** ☉∥♄
♅

February 2023

Monday

3rd Quarter ☾ 8:00am

☽ ♐ **13** ♀♆☿♇♇
5:30pm   ☉□☾
       ♄

3:51pm - 5:30pm

Tuesday

Valentine's Day

☽ ♐ **14** ☿♃
       ♂

Wednesday

E   ♄   ☉✶☾
☽ ♑ **15**   ♀∥♆
8:59pm   ♀☌♆
      ♆♀

5:05pm - 8:59pm

Thursday

F   ♅
☽ ♑ **16**   ☉☌♄
     ♃

February 13 thru 19

Friday

☽ ≈ **17** ♆♀♇ ☿✶♃
9:34pm

8:17pm - 9:34pm

Saturday

☉ Enters ♓ 2:35pm

G ♃♇☿♂
☽ ≈ **18**
♅

Maha Shivaratri
Isra and Mi'raj

Sunday

New ☽ 11:06pm 01° ♓
♀ Enters ♈ 11:55pm

H ☿♄ ☉♂☽
☽ ♓ **19** ♀✶♇
8:55pm

6:00pm - 8:55pm

February 2023

Monday
President's Day

☽ ♓ **20** ♄♅ ☉∥☽
         ♂

Tuesday
Mardi Gras

☽ ♈ **21** ♆♃♇
9:13pm   ☿□♅

8:05pm - 9:13pm

Wednesday
Ash Wednesday

Ⅰ ♀♀♃♃
☽ ♈ **22** ☿△♂

Thursday

♂☿♄
☽ ♈ **23**
      ♇

11:21pm ----------

February 20 thru 26

Friday

J ☽ ♉ **24** ☼ ⚹ ☽
12:28am   ⛢

--------- 12:28am

Saturday

☽ ♉ **25**
☿

⛢ ♆

Sunday

☽ ♊ **26** ♇
7:47am ♄

6:42am - 7:47am

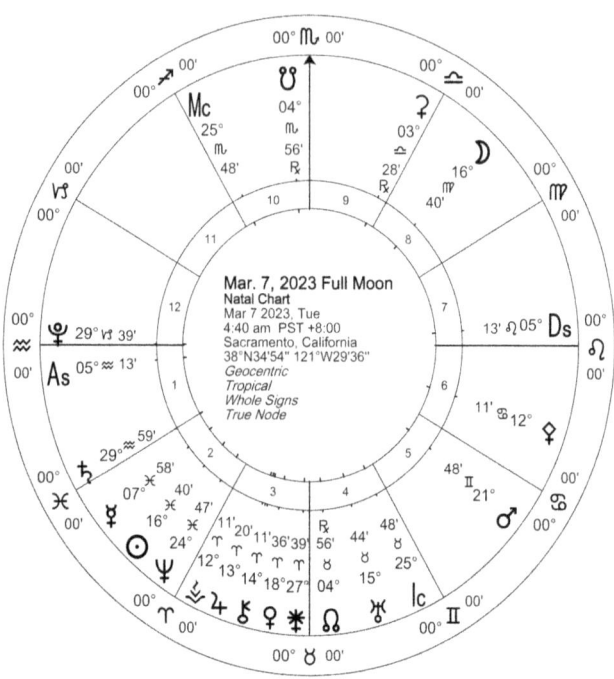

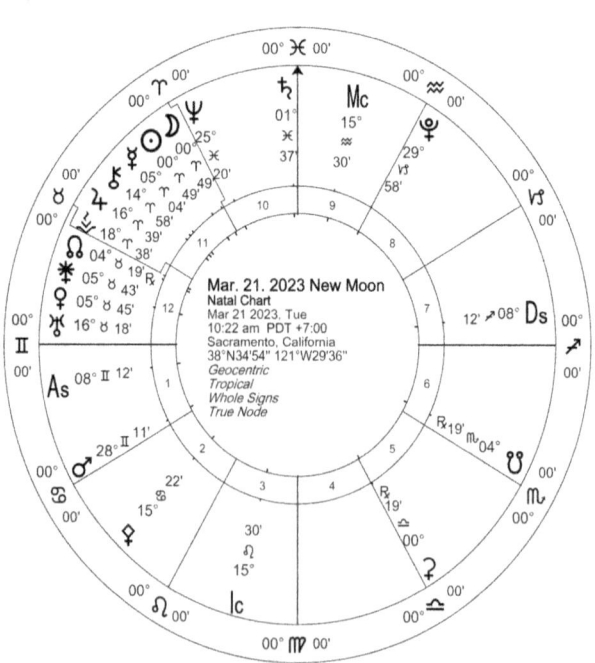

March Forecasts
With Annotated Footnotes (A)
♓ Pisces the Fishes to ♈ Aries the Ram

(A) With Mercury leaving brilliant, airy Aquarius for imaginative Pisces, don't be surprised if your thoughts wander. Your mind likely needs playtime. Energy is rising towards the Full Moon.

(B) This is a momentous day when Saturn enters Pisces after two and a half eventful years in its Ruling Masculine Sign of Aquarius. Saturn in Pisces is less ambitious about career issues, and more focused on promoting spiritual, creative lives and meaningful contributions. This is complicated because repressive Saturn joins expansive Neptune at the Pisces/Virgo Full Moon with Mars in Gemini showing a shift towards the Mutable Signs that have human priorities. Pisces, Virgo, Gemini and Sagittarius will feel this strongly.

(C) This White Circle Day is a welcome breath in after the recent Full Moon. Your interaction with your intimate circle may result in deeper emotional connections. Very interesting for Scorpio.

(D) Thanks to the empowering Sun Trine Moon in Water Signs, supported by Neptune and Pluto, you should make time for activities that make you feel good because the coming week is filled with Astrological tumult.

(E) Prepare for chaos today. The Sun Square Moon does nothing to calm down Mars and Neptune's philosophic arguments, which could spill into emotionally uncomfortable areas for the Mutable Signs.

(F) Everybody wants your attention today, and peacekeepers are nowhere to be seen. The Capricorn Moon lacks the cushiness that might buffer us from the noise. On top of that, Venus enters its Feminine Ruling Sign, Taurus, and she may be a little miffed that her entrance is overshadowed by the chaos. However, she does promise better times to come.

(G) As Venus settles in, make some rules that will protect the simple pleasures of life, a good meal, music and of course, enjoying friends and nature. Give them the priority they deserve. You will get the greatest benefit from this White Circle Day by drawing clear lines around what matters in your life.

(H) After a quick trip through dreamy Pisces, Mercury enters feisty but creative Aries. This is a good time to start new intellectual projects, as well as things that you do with your hands. Watch for new ideas popping up for Aries, Leo & Sagittarius.

(I) Welcome to the Spring Equinox, although with the Moon in Pisces it may feel like Winter is clinging to your coat tails, not wanting to let go. Don't worry, tomorrow's New Moon at zero degrees Aries will take care of that pesky hanger-on.

(J) This is a particularly upbeat New Moon in Aries taking place so early in the Sign, giving a feeling of hope. Combined with a very short Void of Course and a Lunar Conjunction with Mercury, it's okay if you feel younger. Revel in that!

(K) This is the second momentous Planetary Ingress in March, when Pluto enters Aquarius. Astrologers are going to be talking about the significance of this for a while. The last time Pluto entered Aquarius was 245 years ago in 1778. This was a pivotal time during the Revolutionary War. Rather than thinking of this like the Civil War, remember that this was a time when people were actively discussing the importance of participatory governance. Aquarius Sun, Moon and Ascending folks, prepare for Pluto to eventually come visit, at a glacial pace.

(L) Mars moves into Cancer so this is a good time to start home improvement projects. Although Cancers should watch their tempers and any tendency to be impulsive.

(M & N) These two White Circle Days are blessed with personal, social Aspects heralding an easy week which is a nice change after this exciting month. Gemini enjoy!

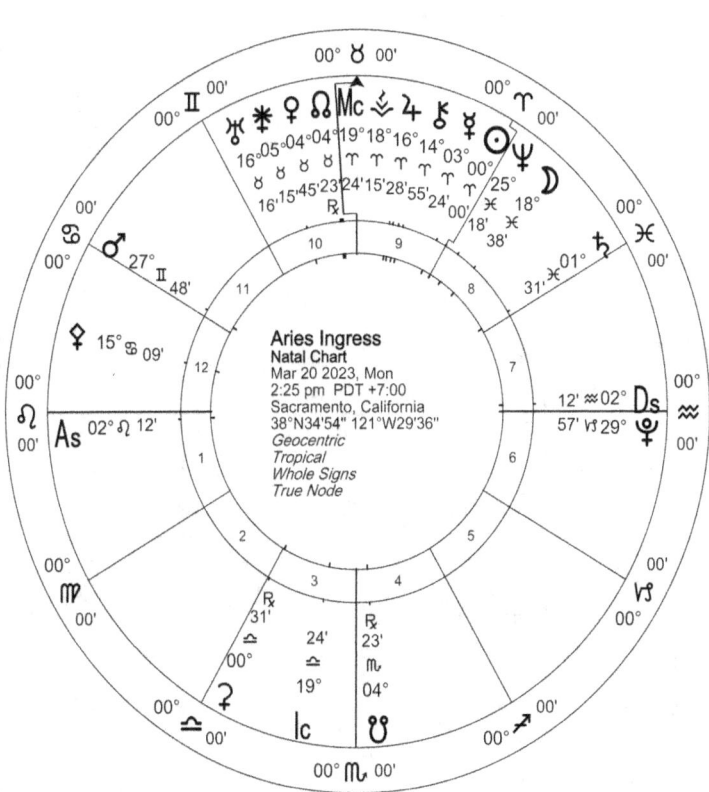

Signs

♈ Aries Begins
♉ Taurus Owns
♊ Gemini Engages
♋ Cancer Nurtures
♌ Leo Embraces
♍ Virgo Improves
♎ Libra Commits
♏ Scorpio Manages
♐ Sagittarius Views
♑ Capricorn Climbs
♒ Aquarius Herds
♓ Pisces Dreams

Planets

☉ Sun Spirit
☽ Moon Emotes
☿ Mercury Thinks
♀ Venus Feels
♂ Mars Acts
♃ Jupiter Expands
♄ Saturn Contracts
♅ Uranus Disrupts
♆ Neptune Envisions
♇ Pluto Unearths

Aspects

☌ Conjunct 0° Aligns
∥ Parallel 0° Equals
✶ Sextile 60° Helps
□ Square 90° Works
△ Trine 120° Supports
☍ Opposition 180° Counters

Visionary Pisces says "I Believe"

Astro Notes:

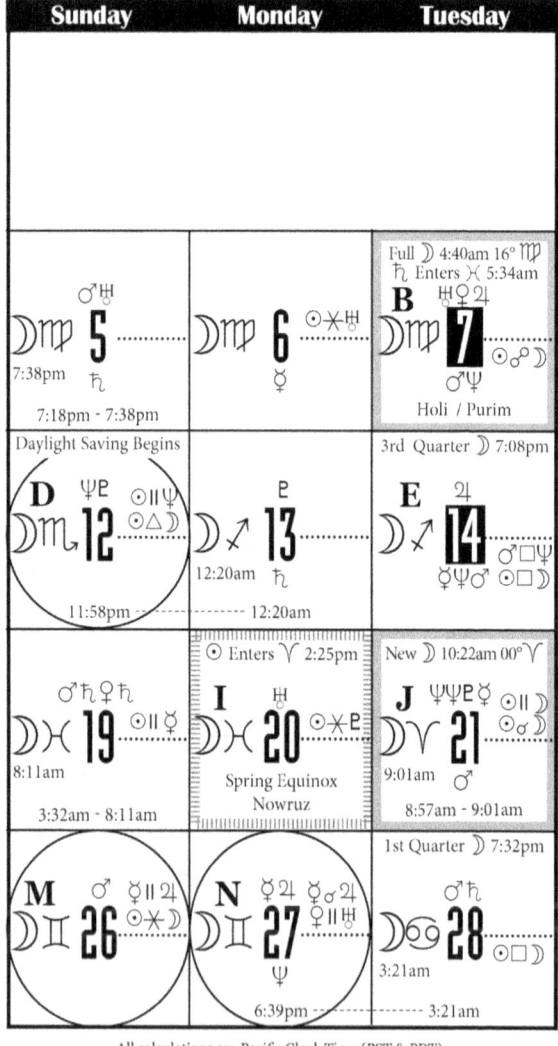

All calculations are Pacific Clock Time (PST & PDT)

Mercury☿ 27° Aquarius♒ enters Pisces♓ on the 2nd at 2:51pm, enters Aries♈ on the 18th at 9:23pm. Venus♀ 11° Aries♈ enters Taurus♉ on the 16th at 3:33pm. Mars♂ 19° Gemini♊ enters Cancer♋ on the 25th at 4:45am. Jupiter♃ 11° Aries♈. Saturn♄ 29° Aquarius♒ enters Pisces♓ on the 7th at 5:34am. Uranus♅ 15° Taurus♉. Neptune♆ 24° Pisces♓. Pluto♇ 29° Capricorn♑ enters Aquarius♒ on the 23rd at 5:14am.

Wednesday	Thursday	Friday	Saturday
♀☌♃ ☉△☽ ☽♋ 1 ♀♃	☿ Enters ♓ 2:51pm A ♅♆ ☽♋ 2 ☿☌♄	♂ ☽♌ 3 ☿∥♄ 7:15am ♇ 6:22am - 7:15am	♃♀ ☽♌ 4 ♅
♇ ☽♎ 8 6:43am 6:07am - 6:43am	♆ ☽♎ 9 ☉∥☽ ♃	♂☿♄♄ ☽♏ 10 4:05pm ♀♇ 3:36pm - 4:05pm	C ☿ ☿⚹♅ ♀⚹♂ ☽♏ 11 ♅
♀♄ ☽♑ 15 ☉☌♆ 5:05am 1:49am - 5:05am	♀ Enters ♉ 3:33pm F ♅♆ ☿∥♆ ☿☌♆ ☽♑ 16 ☉□♂ ♃ ♀□♇ ☿□♂	St. Patrick's Day G ☿♇ ♀⚹♄ ☉☌☿ ☽♒ 17 ☉⚹☽ 7:24am ♀ 7:13am - 7:24am	☿ Enters ♈ 9:23pm H ♇♃ ☽♒ 18 ☿⚹♇ ♅
☿♃♃ ☽♈ 22	♇ Enters ♒ 5:14am Ramadan K ♂♄ ☽♉ 23 11:41am ♇ 10:12am - 11:41am	♀♀♅♅ ☽♉ 24	♂ Enters ♋ 4:45am L ♆♇ ☽♊ 25 5:41pm ♄ 9:18am - 5:41pm
♀♅ ☽♋ 29 ♃☿	♆♂ ♀☌♅ ☽♌ 30 ♂△♄ 3:31pm ♇ 6:45am - 3:31pm	☽♌ 31 ☉△☽	

Add 1 Hour for Mountain Time (MT) - Add 2 Hours for Central Time (CT) - Add 3 Hours for Eastern Time (ET)

March 2023

Monday
1st Quarter ☾ 12:05am

☾ ♊ **27** ♀♃♂♂
⊙□☾

Tuesday

☾♋ **28** ☿♄ ♀∥♃
6:39pm ♆
5:07pm - 6:39pm

Wednesday

☾♋ **1** ♀♂♃
⊙△☾
♀♃

Thursday
☿ Enters ♓ 2:51pm

A ♅♆
☾♋ **2** ☿♂♄

February 27 thru March 5

Friday

☽♌ **3** ☿∥♄
7:15am ♂
         ♀

6:22am - 7:15am

Saturday

☽♌ **4** ♃♀
         ♅

Sunday

☽♍ **5** ♂♅
7:38pm ♄

7:18pm - 7:38pm

March 2023

Monday

☽♍ **6** ☉✶♅
 ☿

Tuesday

Full ☽ 4:40am 16° ♍
♄ Enters ♓ 5:34am
B ♅♀♃
☽♍ **7** ☉☍☽
 ♂♆
Holi / Purim

Wednesday

☽♎ **8** ♇
6:43am
6:07am - 6:43am

Thursday

☽♎ **9** ♆ ☉♊☽
 ♃

March 6 thru 12

Friday

☽♏ **10** ♂☿♄♄
4:05pm   ♀♇

3:36pm - 4:05pm

Saturday

C ☽♏ **11** ☿ ☿⚹♅
♀⚹♂
♅°

Sunday
Daylight Saving Begins

D ☽♏ **12** ♆♇   ☉∥♆
☉△☽

11:58pm

March 2023

Monday

☽ ♐ **13** ᴾ
12:20am ♄
------- 12:20am

Tuesday
3rd Quarter ☽ 7:08pm

☽ ♐ **14** ᴱ ♃
♂□♆
☿♆♂ ☉□☽

Wednesday

☽ ♑ **15** ♀♄ ☉☌♆
5:05am
1:49am - 5:05am

Thursday
♀ Enters ♉ 3:33pm

☽ ♑ **16** ᶠ ♅♆ ☿∥♆
☿☌♆
☉□♂
♃ ♀□ᴾ
☿□♂

March 13 thru 19

Friday
St. Patrick's Day

G ☿ ♇ ♀✶♄
☽≈ **17** ☉♂☿
7:24am ♀ ☉✶☽

7:13am - 7:24am

Saturday
☿ Enters ♈ 9:23pm

H ♇ ♃
☽≈ **18** ☿✶♇
♅

Sunday

♂♄♀♄
☽♓ **19** ☉∥☿
8:11am

3:32am - 8:11am

March 2023

Monday
☉ Enters ♈ 2:25pm

I
☽♓ **20** ⛢̊ ☉✶♇

Spring Equinox
Nowruz

Tuesday
New ☽ 10:22am 00°♈

J ♆♇☿ ☉♊☽
☽♈ **21**
9:01am ♂
8:57am - 9:01am

Wednesday

☿♃♃
☽♈ **22**

Thursday
♇ Enters ♒ 5:14am
Ramadan

K ♂♄
☽♉ **23**
11:41am ♇
10:12am - 11:41am

March 20 thru 26

	Friday ♀♀♅♅ ☽♉ **24**
L	**Saturday** ♂ Enters ♋ 4:45am L ♆♇ ☽♊ **25** 5:41pm ♄ 9:18am - 5:41pm
M	**Sunday** M ♂ ☿∥♃ ☽♊ **26** ☉⚹☽

March into April 2023

Monday
☽ N ♊ **27** ☿♃ ☿☌♃ ♀∥♅ ♆
6:39pm

Tuesday
1st Quarter ☽ 7:32pm

☽ ☽♋ **28** ♂♄ ☉□☽
3:21am

------- 3:21am

Wednesday
☽ ☽♋ **29** ♀♅ ♃ ☿

Thursday
☽ ☽♌ **30** ♆♂ ♀☌♅ ♂△♄ ♇
3:31pm
6:45am - 3:31pm

March 27 thru April 2

Friday

☽♌ **31** ☉△☽

Saturday

♃☿
☽♌ **1**
♅♀
11:02pm

Sunday
Palm Sunday

♅☿
☽♍ **2**
3:57am ♄♂
-------- 3:57am

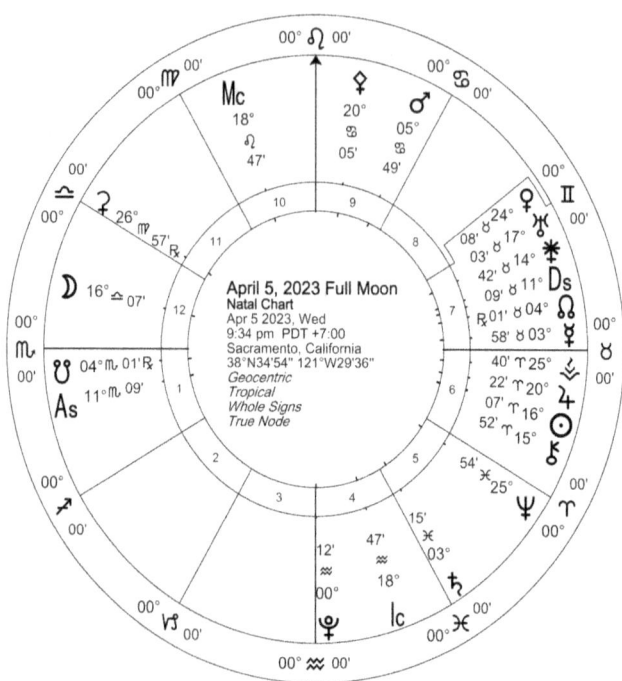

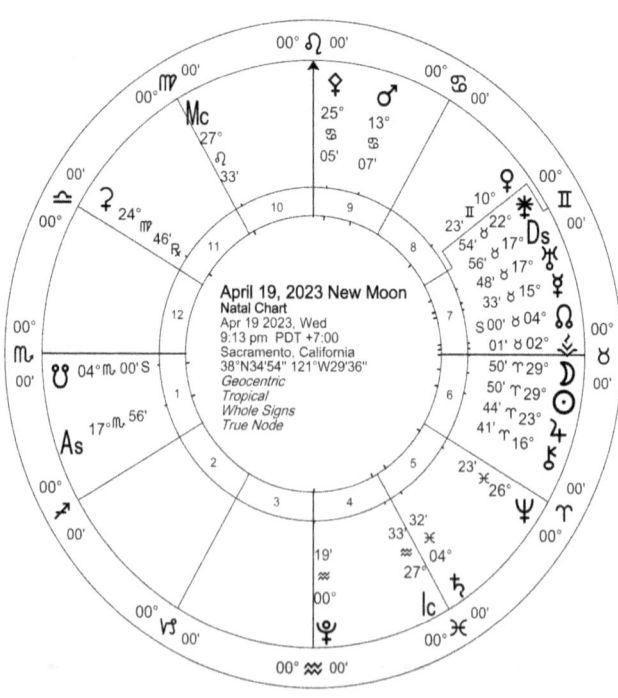

April Forecasts
With Annotated Footnotes (A)
♈ Aries the Ram to ♉ Taurus the Bull

While March experienced plenty of Sign changes, April only sees Mercury and Venus shift, but Mercury is slowing to turn Retrograde on the 21st. While the other Planets moving Direct encourage smooth progress, the New Moon Eclipse on the 19th will complicate the end of the month. Read (F) & (I) carefully.

(A) Mercury moves into Taurus so expect a little turbulence that day, but the mental pace slows to a more graceful rhythm. Mentally good for the Earth Signs, Taurus, Virgo and Capricorn, challenging to Scorpio.

(B) The Libra/Aries Full Moon happening with Mercury Sextile Saturn creates a good window for forming practical partnerships. Aries, Libra, Cancer and Capricorn will feel challenged, but use the energy to achieve your goals. Good for Gemini and Sagittarius.

(C) The long Void of Course Libra Moon can be distracting so make a conservative list of what you need to accomplish today.

(D) This day moves along smoothly with an easy interaction among your intimates. A good day to seek out people of authority with leverage over issues that matter to you. Scorpio prepare for an emotional day.

(E) Venus moves from graceful Taurus into playful Gemini so stretch your conversation and flirting skills because they will be quite helpful going forward. Good for the Air Signs.

(F) Big Event! As the Sun Conjuncts Jupiter in Aries there will be a burst of creative energy available so the Aries Sun people will feel powered up, but wherever you have Aries in your chart can expand optimistically. Also good for Leo and Sagittarius.

(G & H) A pair of Black Boxes can prove challenging, so don't plan on coasting. It will take serious work to accomplish what you aim to do.

(I) Big Event! This Eclipse at the last degree of Aries starts a two-week period until the Full Moon on May 5th that can be emotionally complex and at times difficult. Fortunately, it carries the optimism of the recent Sun Jupiter Conjunction, but with multiple Planets in Taurus, use this time to ground yourself in nature. Those born late in Aries and early in Taurus take care.

(J) The Sun enters Taurus and the middle part of Spring when the bounty of nature appears. With Sun Square Pluto newly in Aquarius, issues of nature versus technology may arise.

(K) Mercury turns Retrograde in the middle of Taurus. It complicates the message of the Eclipse but speaks about the recent changes in Sign of Saturn and Pluto. Use this time to review changes in your life. Taurus and Scorpio, be careful around electricity.

(L) This White Circle Day can help you accomplish significant things but be prepared to innovate. Especially you, Cancer!

(M) The month ends with a practical and smooth White Circle Day perfect for buying plants or working in the garden. Good for the Earth Signs and especially for Taurus and Virgo.

Eclipses are important events, and it is helpful to know where it takes place in your own Chart. If it lands on a major Planet, it will affect your perception of the world. If it lands on any of the Angles, Ascendant, Midheaven, Descendant or IC, it can signify a change in direction in that part of your life.

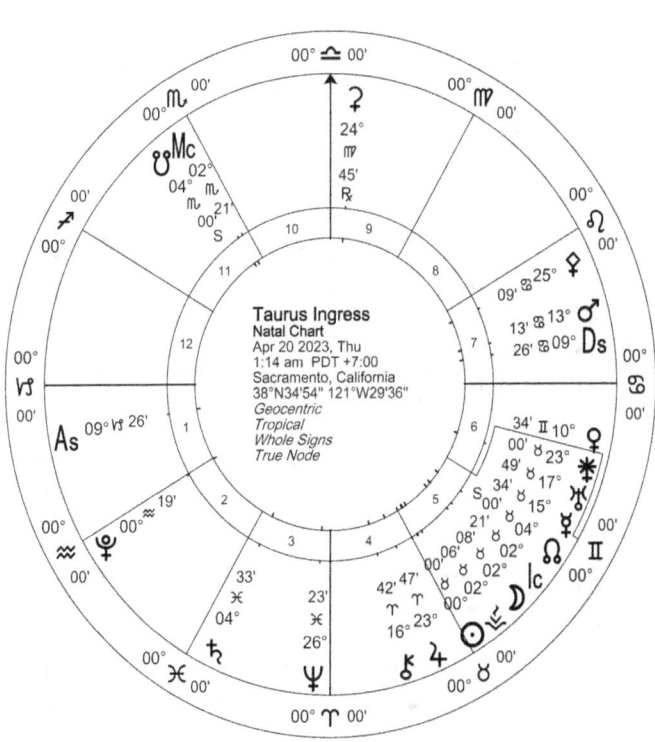

Signs

♈ Aries Begins
♉ Taurus Owns
♊ Gemini Engages
♋ Cancer Nurtures
♌ Leo Embraces
♍ Virgo Improves
♎ Libra Commits
♏ Scorpio Manages
♐ Sagittarius Views
♑ Capricorn Climbs
♒ Aquarius Herds
♓ Pisces Dreams

Planets

☉ Sun Spirit
☽ Moon Emotes
☿ Mercury Thinks
♀ Venus Feels
♂ Mars Acts
♃ Jupiter Expands
♄ Saturn Contracts
♅ Uranus Disrupts
♆ Neptune Envisions
♇ Pluto Unearths

Aspects

☌ Conjunct 0° Aligns
∥ Parallel 0° Equals
✶ Sextile 60° Helps
□ Square 90° Works
△ Trine 120° Supports
☍ Opposition 180° Counters

Energetic Aries says "I Act"

Astro Notes:

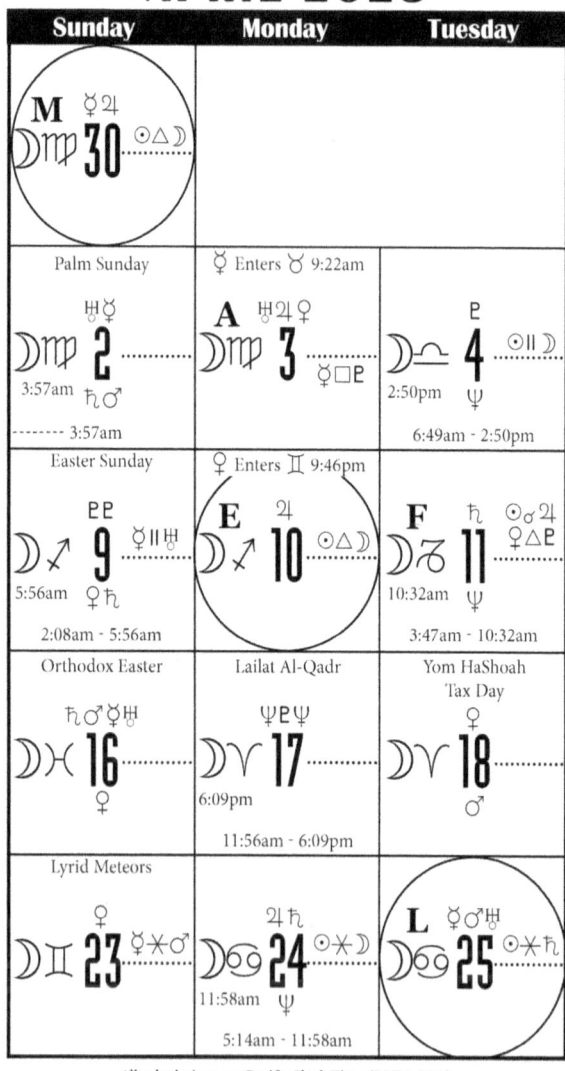

All calculations are Pacific Clock Time (PST & PDT)

Mercury☿ 25° Aries♈ enters Taurus♉ on the 3rd at 9:22am, turns Rx on the 21st at 1:34am at 15° Taurus♉. Venus♀ 18° Taurus♉ enters Gemini♊ on the 10th at 9:46pm. Mars♂ 3° Cancer♋. Jupiter♃ 19° Aries♈. Saturn♄ 02° Pisces♓. Uranus♅ 16° Taurus♉. Neptune♆ 25° Pisces♓. Pluto♇ 00° Aquarius♒.

Wednesday	Thursday	Friday	Saturday
			♃☿ ☽♌ 1 ♅♀ 11:02pm
Full ☽ 9:34pm 16° ♎ B ♆ ☽♎ 5 ☿✶♄ ☉☍☽ ♂	Passover First Day C ☽♏ 6 11:29pm ♃♇ 5:42am - 11:29pm	Good Friday D ♄♄♂ ☽♏ 7 ☿✶♂ ♀✶♆ ☿	♆ ☽♏ 8 ☉∥♃ ♅
☿♅ ☽♑ 12 ♂	3rd Quarter ☽ 2:11am Passover Ends G ♆♇♀ ☽♒ 13 ☉□☽ 1:41pm ♃ 7:13am - 1:41pm	Orthodox Good Friday H ♇ ☽♒ 14 ♀□♄ ☿♅	♃♄ ☽♓ 15 ☉✶☽ 3:56pm 8:15am - 3:56pm
New ☽ 9:13pm 29° ♈ ☉ Hybrid Eclipse I ♃♃ ☉∥☽ ☽♉ 19 ☉☌☽ 9:29pm ♇ 9:12pm - 9:29pm	☉ Enters ♉ 1:14am J ♄♂♅ ☽♉ 20 ☉□♇	Eid Al-Fitr Begins K ☿♅☿♆ ☽♉ 21 ☿Rx 8:40pm	Earth Day Lyrid Meteors ♇♂♀ ☽♊ 22 ♀∥♂ 3:10am ♄ 3:10am
Yom Ha'atzmaut ♆ ☽♌ 26 11:29pm ♃ 4:40pm - 11:29pm	1st Quarter ☽ 2:19pm ♀♂ ☽♌ 27 ☉□☽ ♇	National Arbor Day ♀ ☽♌ 28 ☿♅	☉∥☽ ♃♅☿ ♂✶♅ ☽♍ 29 ☿∥♅ 11:58am ♄ 3:52am - 11:58am

Add 1 Hour for Mountain Time (MT) - Add 2 Hours for Central Time (CT) - Add 3 Hours for Eastern Time (ET)

April 2023

Monday
☿ Enters ♉ 9:22am

A ♅♃♀
☽♍ **3**
☿□♇

Tuesday

☽♎ **4** ☉∥☽
2:50pm ♇
♆

6:49am - 2:50pm

Wednesday
Full ☽ 9:34pm 16° ♎

B ♆ ☿✶♄
☽♎ **5** ☉☍☽
♂

Thursday
Passover First Day

C
☽♏ **6**
11:29pm ♃♇

5:42am - 11:29pm

April 3 thru 9

Friday
Good Friday

D ♄ ♄ ♂ ☿⚹♂
☽♏ 7   ♀⚹♆
         ☿

Saturday

     ♆
☽♏ 8   ☉∥♃
     ♅

Sunday
Easter Sunday

          ᴘᴘ
☽♐ 9   ☿∥♅
5:56am ♀♄
2:08am - 5:56am

April 2023

Monday
♀ Enters ♊ 9:46pm

E
☽♐ 10 ♃ ☉△☽

Tuesday
F
☽♑ 11 ♄ ☉☌♃
    ♀△♇
10:32am ♆

3:47am - 10:32am

Wednesday
☽♑ 12 ☿♅
    ♂

Thursday
3rd Quarter ☽ 2:11am
Passover Ends

G
☽♒ 13 ♆♇♀
1:41pm ☉□☽
    ♃

7:13am - 1:41pm

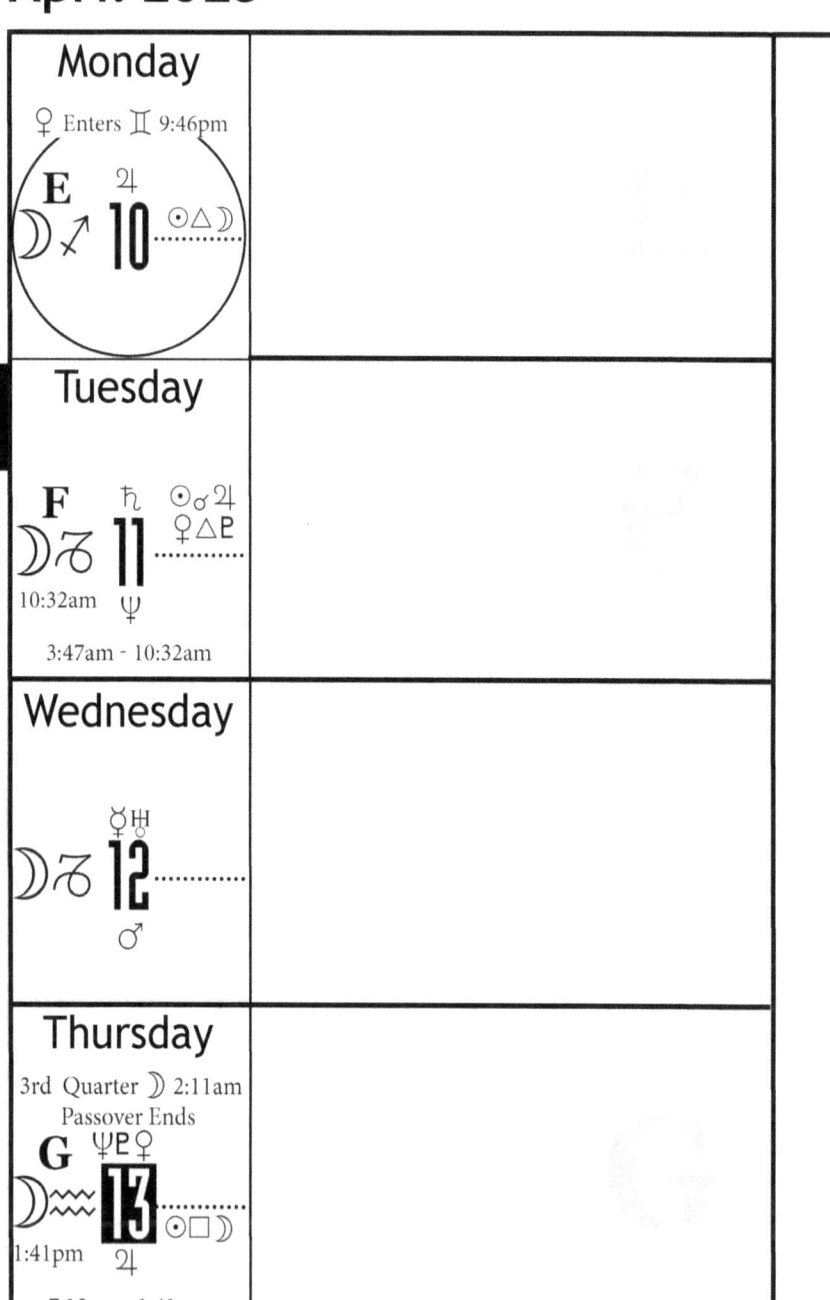

April 10 thru 16

Friday
Orthodox Good Friday

☾♒ **14** ♇♅
H ♀□♄
☿♅

Saturday

☾♓ **15** ♃♄ ☉✶☾
3:56pm

8:15am - 3:56pm

Sunday
Orthodox Easter

♄☌☿♅
☾♓ **16**
♀

75

April 2023

Monday
Lailat Al-Qadr

☽ ♈ ♆♇♆ **17**
6:09pm

11:56am - 6:09pm

Tuesday
Yom HaShoah
Tax Day

☽ ♈ ♀ **18** ♂

Wednesday

New ☽ 9:13pm 29° ♈
☉ Hybrid Eclipse
I ♃ ☉‖☽
☽ ♉ **19** ☉☌☽
9:29pm ♇

9:12pm - 9:29pm

Thursday
☉ Enters ♉ 1:14am

J ♄♂♅
☽ ♉ **20** ☉□♇

April 17 thru 23

Friday
Eid Al-Fitr Begins

K ☿↯♅☿♆
☽♉ **21** ☿Rx

8:40pm

Saturday
Earth Day
Lyrid Meteors

♇♂♀
☽♊ **22** ♀∥♂
3:10am ♄

---------3:10am

Sunday
Lyrid Meteors

♀
☽♊ **23** ☿✶♂

April 2023

Monday

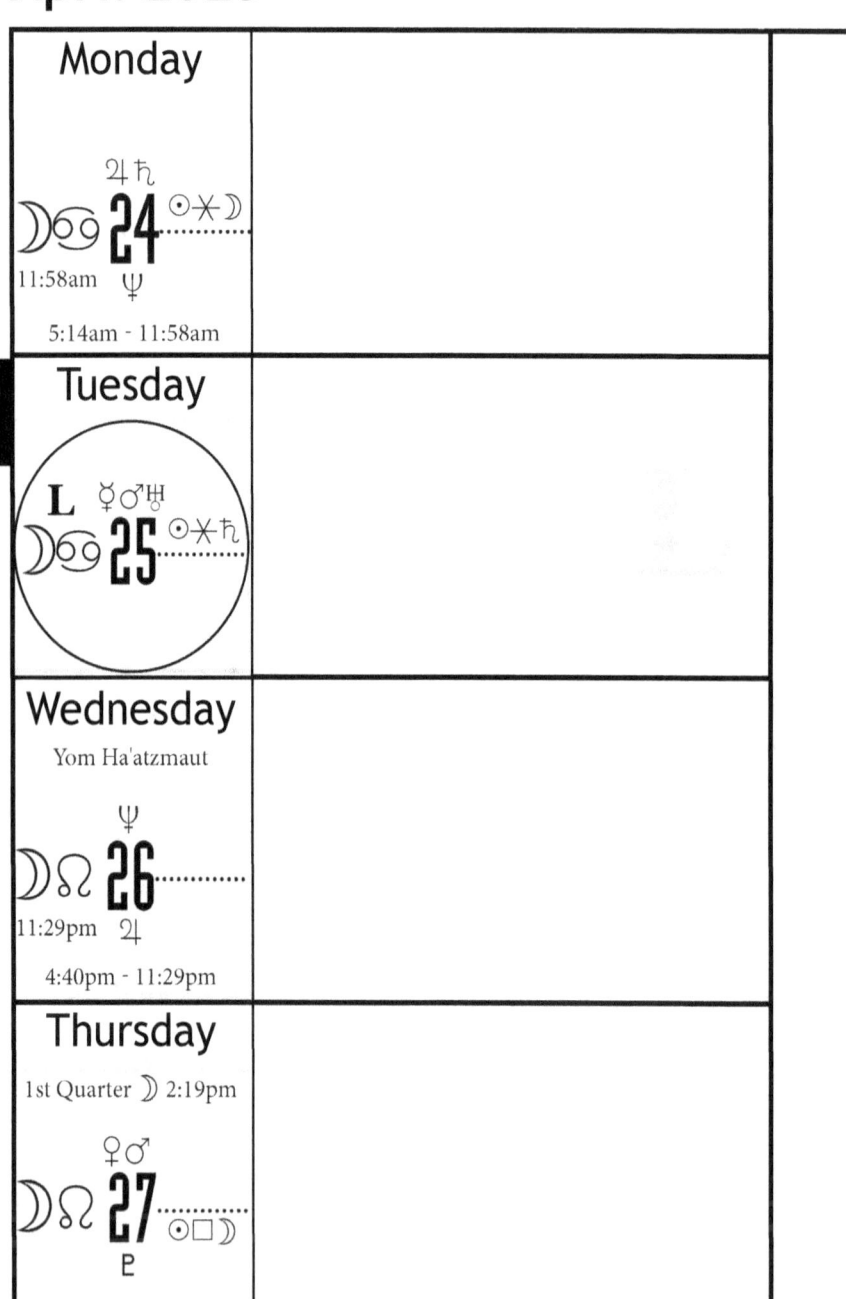

☽♋ **24** ☉✶☽
11:58am ♃♄
       ♆

5:14am - 11:58am

Tuesday

L ☿♂♅
☽♋ **25** ☉✶♄

Wednesday

Yom Ha'atzmaut

       ♆
☽♌ **26**
11:29pm ♃

4:40pm - 11:29pm

Thursday

1st Quarter ☽ 2:19pm

     ♀♂
☽♌ **27** ☉□☽
     ♇

April 24 thru 30

Friday
National Arbor Day

☽ ♌ **28** ♀⇡ ☿♅⇣

Saturday

☽ ♍ **29** ♃♅☿ ♂⚹♅ ☉∥☽ ☿∥♅
11:58am ♄

3:52am - 11:58am

Sunday

M ☿♃
☽♍ **30** ☉△☽

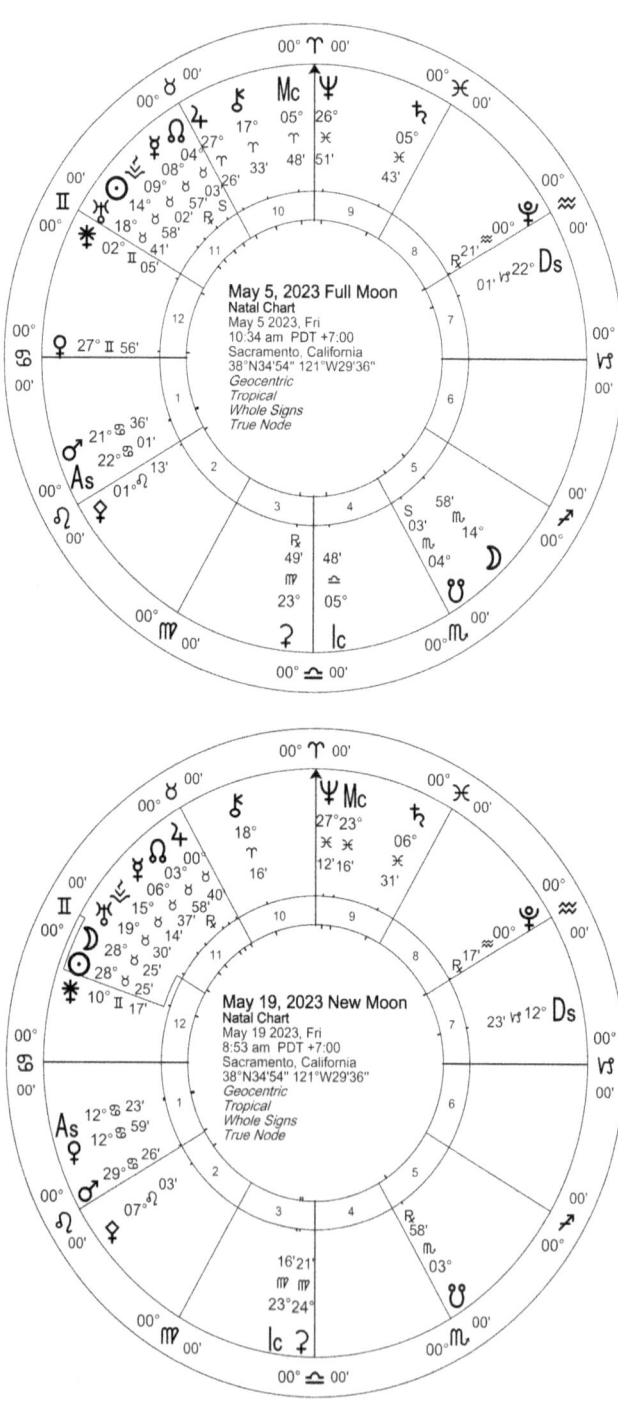

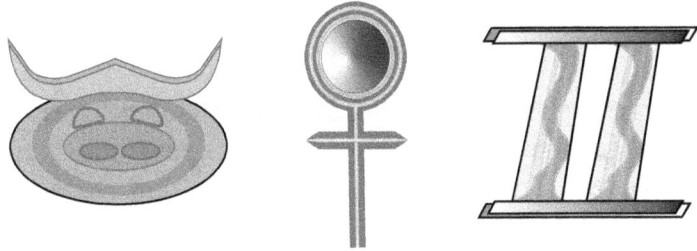

May Forecasts
With Annotated Footnotes (A)
♉ Taurus the Bull to ♊ Gemini the Twins

The first week of this month is the wind down of the year's first Eclipse pair, so expect to feel some emotional intensity until the fifth. But soon after that Venus enters Cancer which pairs beautifully with the Taurus Sun to help us feel grounded and cared for. Then Mercury turns Direct so everything will begin to smooth out. When Jupiter enters Taurus soon after, followed by Mars entering Leo, it will feel like a page has been turned.

(A) Pluto, newly in Aquarius, turns Retrograde. Don't expect to feel it too personally, but there will be gradual effects in the outer world that we will likely talk about in the video forecast.

(B) Big Event. The emotionally complicated two weeks between Eclipses concludes with the Full Moon on the 5th. Taurus and Scorpio should guard against emotional upset and feeling forgotten.

(C) Venus moves from flirty Gemini to cushy Cancer so, when you want to express love to others, feed them. Cancer, watch out for overindulgence at the dinner table. In this pause after the Eclipse, allow yourself emotional space for processing.

(D) The Sun Conjunct Uranus is a day with sizzle that will leak out into the days before and after. Watch for freak events in the news and guard against them in your personal life. Taurus should be especially careful.

(E) This complex day at the third quarter Moon includes multiple supportive personal Planet Aspects. Expect things to shift as people who were less open to connections start responding to your overtures.

(F) On Mother's Day, Mercury in Taurus turns Direct with the Sun Sextile the Moon, and good Lunar Aspects making this an especially charming day for a celebration. Choose unusual gifts, although wine is almost always welcome.

(G) Big Event! Jupiter raced through energetic Aries and enters placid practical Taurus, so expect the two halves of the month, and the year, to have different themes. For the rest of the year, those with strong Taurus will find their horizons expanded so enjoy that. Where is Taurus in your chart? Because that area wants to grow!

(H) The White Circle Day on the 18th is packed full of exciting Aspects so any project you start at this time will get a bit of extra juice. Good for both the Earth and Water Signs.

(I) The Taurus New Moon happens at the Pleiades Constellation, near Uranus and Sextile Mars at the last degree of Cancer. There is the potential for emotional outbursts. But that's okay if it gets the attention of those who need to listen.

(J) Mars leaves cushy Cancer for Leo, so drama and stage craft become the name of the game. Leos watch out about overdoing it physically as well as bumping your head, as Mars makes you more impulsive.

(K) The Sun enters intellectual Gemini while making a Sextile to Mars and a Trine to Pluto, while Jupiter Sextiles the Moon late in the day. There is a great deal of power in this day along with a good bit of drama and fun. Very stimulating for the Air Signs, Gemini, Libra and Aquarius!

(L) Watch out because Mars is exactly Square Jupiter, and the work ahead may look overwhelming. Relax, great works are accomplished in little bits. The rest of the week is pleasantly mild, a nice change after the barrage of Transits midmonth. The Fixed Signs will feel it most!

(M) Use that Sun Trine Moon to move things along because resistance will be moderate and quickly dispersed, energizing for the Air Signs!

Look at where Aries and Taurus are in your chart, because Jupiter changing Signs will shift your focus in significant ways. If you have major Planets or Angles in those Signs the effects will be more obvious.

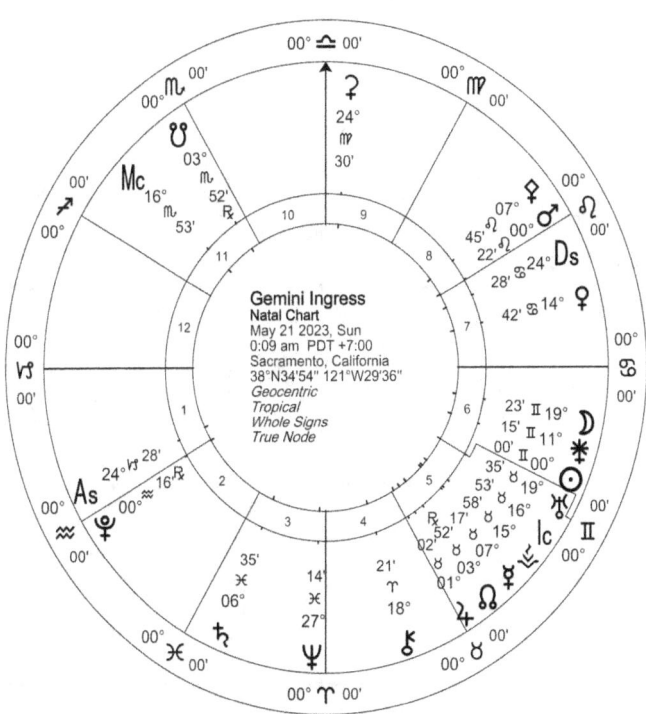

Signs

♈ Aries Begins
♉ Taurus Owns
♊ Gemini Engages
♋ Cancer Nurtures
♌ Leo Embraces
♍ Virgo Improves
♎ Libra Commits
♏ Scorpio Manages
♐ Sagittarius Views
♑ Capricorn Climbs
♒ Aquarius Herds
♓ Pisces Dreams

Planets

☉ Sun Spirit
☽ Moon Emotes
☿ Mercury Thinks
♀ Venus Feels
♂ Mars Acts
♃ Jupiter Expands
♄ Saturn Contracts
♅ Uranus Disrupts
♆ Neptune Envisions
♇ Pluto Unearths

Aspects

☌ Conjunct 0° Aligns
∥ Parallel 0° Equals
⚹ Sextile 60° Helps
□ Square 90° Works
△ Trine 120° Supports
☍ Opposition 180° Counters

Sensual Taurus says "I Possess"

Astro Notes:

MAY 2023

Sunday	Monday	Tuesday
	May Day / Lei Day **A** ☽♎ **1** ♅☌♇ ☉☌☿ ♇Rx 11:08pm ♀♆ 4:52pm - 11:08pm	☽♎ **2** ♆ ☉∥♉
♀ Enters ♋ 7:24am / Eta Aquarid Meteors **C** ☽♐ **7**	☽♑ **8** ♃ ☉∥♅ 4:32pm ♅♀ 1:27pm - 4:32pm	Lag BaOmer **D** ☽♑ **9** ♄♀ ☉☌♅ ♃ Enters ♉ 10:19am
Mother's Day **F** ♅☌♆ ♀'D' ☽♓ **14** ☉⚹☽ 7:56pm	☽♈ **15** ♇♆ ♂△♆ 12:55am ♀ 12:55am	**G** ☽♈ **16**
☉ Enters ♊ 12:09am **K** ♃☉⚹♂ ☽♋ **21** ☉△♇ 8:28pm ♆ 3:11pm - 8:28pm	**L** ☽♋ **22** ♄♀ ♂□♃	☽♋ **23** ♀♅ ☿∥♃
☽♍ **28** ♅♀ ☉□♄	Memorial Day ☽♎ **29** ♇♂ 7:50am ♆ 2:45am - 7:50am	**M** ☽♎ **30** ♆ ☉△☽

All calculations are Pacific Clock Time (PST & PDT)

Mercury☿Rx 11° Taurus♉ turns Direct on the 14th at 8:16pm at 5° Taurus♉. Venus♀ 23° Gemini♊ enters Cancer♋ on the 7th at 7:24am. Mars♂ 19° Cancer♋ enters Leo♌ on the 20th at 8:31am. Jupiter♃ 26° Aries♈ enters Taurus♉ on the 16th at 10:19am. Saturn♄ 05° Pisces♓. Uranus♅ 18° Taurus♉. Neptune♆ 26° Pisces♓. Pluto♇ 00° Aquarius♒ turns Rx on the 1st at 10:08am at 00° Aquarius♒.

Wednesday	Thursday	Friday	Saturday
☽♎ **3** ♂	♀♄♄ ☽♏ **4** ♀⚹♃ ♀□♆ 7:32am ♃♇ 2:16am - 7:32am	Full ☽ 10:34am 14° ♏ Appulse ☾ Eclipse B ♂ ☽♏ **5** ☉☍☽ ☿♅ Cinco de Mayo	Eta Aquarid Meteors Kentucky Derby ♆♇♇ ☽♐ **6** 1:03pm ♄ 7:37am - 1:03pm
♅♆♇ ☽♒ **10** ☉△☽ 7:05pm ♂♃ 4:52pm - 7:05pm	♇ ☽♒ **11** ☿	3rd Quarter ☽ 7:28am E ♃ ♀△♄ ☿⚹♀ ☿⚹♄ ☽♓ **12** ☉□☽ 9:38pm ♅ 8:15pm - 9:38pm	☿♄♀♄ ☽♓ **13**
♃☿♃☿♄ ☽♉ **17** ♃□♇ 5:27am ♂♇ 2:09am - 5:27am	H ♀♅♅ ☿⚹♄ ☉∥☽ ☿∥♃ ☉⚹♆ ☽♉ **18**	New ☽ 8:53am 28°♉ I ♆♂♂♇ ☽♊ **19** ☉☌☽ 11:47am ♄ 10:50am - 11:47am	♂ Enters ♌ 8:31am J ♀ ☽♊ **20** ♂☍♇
♆♀♂ ☽♌ **24** ☉⚹☽ 7:34am ♇♃ 2:11am - 7:34am	♂ ☉∥☽ ☉∥♂ ☽♌ **25** ☿♅ 11:38pm ---------	Shavuot ♅ ☽♍ **26** ♀⚹♅ 8:04pm --------- 8:04pm	1st Quarter ☽ 8:22am ♃☿♃☿ ☽♍ **27** ☉□☽ ♄
♄ ☽♏ **31** 4:44pm ♀♇♃ 7:53am - 4:44pm			

Add 1 Hour for Mountain Time (MT) - Add 2 Hours for Central Time (CT) - Add 3 Hours for Eastern Time (ET)

May 2023

Monday
May Day
Lei Day

A ♅♂♇
☽♎ 1 ☉♂☿
11:08pm   ♇Rx
       ♀♆

4:52pm - 11:08pm

Tuesday

       ♆
☽♎ 2 ☉∥☿

Wednesday

☽♎ 3 ....
      ♂

Thursday

     ♀♄♄
☽♏ 4 ♀⚹♃
7:32am   ♀□♆
      ♃♇

2:16am - 7:32am

May 1 thru 7

Friday

Full ☾ 10:34am 14° ♏
Appulse ☾ Eclipse

B ♂

☾♏ **5** ☉☍☾
☿♁

Cinco de Mayo

Saturday

Eta Aquarid Meteors
Kentucky Derby

♆♇

☾♐ **6**

1:03pm ♄

7:37am - 1:03pm

Sunday

♀ Enters ♋ 7:24am
Eta Aquarid Meteors

C

☾♐ **7**

May 2023

Monday

☽ ♑ ♃ **8** ☉∥♅
4:32pm   ♆♀
1:27pm - 4:32pm

Tuesday
Lag BaOmer

D ♄☿
☽ ♑ **9** ☉☌♅

Wednesday

☽ ♒ ♅♆♇ **10** ☉△☽
7:05pm   ♂♃
4:52pm - 7:05pm

Thursday

☽ ♒ ♇ **11**
  ☿

May 8 thru 14

Friday
3rd Quarter ☾ 7:28am

E

☾ ♓ **12** ♃ ☿ ☿ ⚴ ☉ ♅

9:38pm

♀△♄
☿✶♀
☿✶♄
☉□☾

8:15pm - 9:38pm

Saturday

☿♄ ♀♄

☾ ♓ **13** ············

Sunday
Mother's Day

F ♅☌♆ ☿'D'

☾ ♓ **14** ☉✶♀

7:56pm

89

May 2023

Monday

☽♈ **15** ♂△♆
♇ ♆
12:55am ♀
--------- 12:55am

Tuesday

♃ Enters ♉ 10:19am

G
☽♈ **16** ....

Wednesday

♃ ☿ ♃ ♄
☽♉ **17** ....
5:27am ♂♇ ♃□♇

2:09am - 5:27am

Thursday

H ♀♅♅ ☿✶♄
☽♉ **18** ☉∥☽
☿∥♃
☉✶♆

May 15 thru 21

Friday

New ☽ 8:53am 28° ♉

I ♆☌♂♇
☽♊ **19** ☉☌☽
11:47am ♄
10:50am - 11:47am

Saturday

♂ Enters ♌ 8:31am

J ♀
☽♊ **20**
♂☍♇

Sunday

☉ Enters ♊ 12:09am

K ♃ ☉✶♂
☽♋ **21** ☉△♇
8:28pm ♆
3:11pm - 8:28pm

May 2023

Monday

☽♋ **22** L ♄☿ ♂□♃

Tuesday

☽♋ **23** ♀♅ ☿∥♃

Wednesday

☽♌ **24** ♆♀♂ ☉✶☽
7:34am ♇♃
2:11am - 7:34am

Thursday

☽♌ **25** ♂ ☉∥☽ ☉∥♂ ☿♅
11:38pm ----------

May 22 thru 28

Friday
Shavuot

☽♍ 26 ♀⚹♅
8:04pm
---------- 8:04pm

Saturday
1st Quarter ☽ 8:22am

☽♍ 27 ☉□☽
♄

Sunday

☽♍ 28 ☉□♄

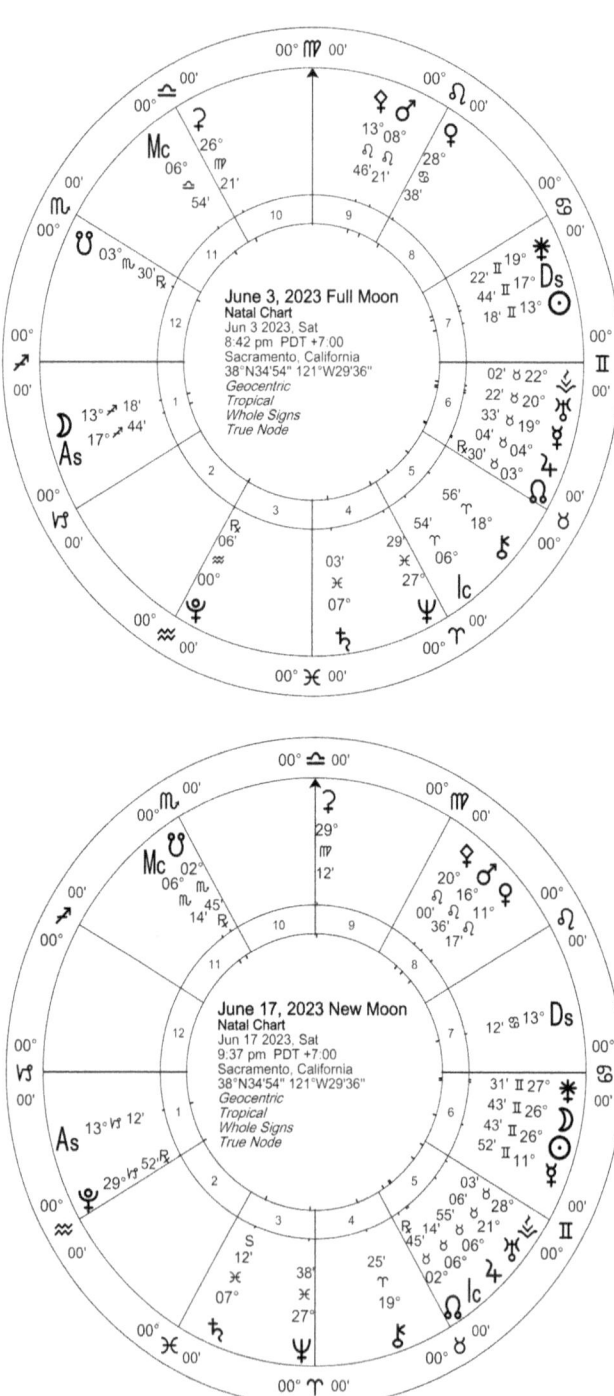

June Forecasts
With Annotated Footnotes (A)
♊ Gemini the Twins to ♋ Cancer the Crab

With Mercury moving fast while Venus moves into the Summertime Signs, personal connections warm up and become more satisfying. Meanwhile, Saturn and Neptune turn Retrograde so events in the outer world may begin to stall. Around June 4th watch for Venus in the western sky at sunset when it will be brilliantly beautiful.

(A) This White Circle Day is due to a lovely Venus Trine Neptune, great for romance, imagination, socializing and dreaming. This is especially helpful for the Water Signs, Cancer, Scorpio and Pisces.

(B) The Full Moon focuses on Gemini and Sagittarius and the Leo Mars adds 'umph' to the mix so wherever those Signs are in your chart will get charged up. Challenging for the Mutable Signs but good for the Fire!

(C) Venus joins Mars in heart centered Leo, so indulge in the scent of roses and romantic comedies to lift the spirits. Leos will feel empowered, as will Aries and Sagittarius.

(D) The Sun Trine the Aquarius Moon following the Full Moon is an excellent time to move projects along to completion, although it may require overcoming petty stubbornness. Great for Gemini, Libra and Aquarius.

(E) The White Circle Day enjoys a Mercury Sextile Neptune making it easy to communicate ideas from your imagination about your vision for the future. With Saturn and Jupiter helping the Moon there is emotional power behind your ideas. Good for Cancer, Scorpio and Pisces.

(F) Pluto backs into Capricorn while Mercury enters its Ruling Sign Gemini, so while there may be mild backsliding in global issues, personal communication will clarify and accelerate during the Gemini Transit.

(G) With so many Lunar Aspects happening, Mercury Square Saturn, and both Mercury and Venus demanding attention, watch out for getting overcommitted or overstimulated. Taurus beware, forget the news and turn on your music.

(H) The New Moon in late Gemini happens coincidentally with a friendly Sextile between Mercury and Venus encouraging social engagement and flirting. Saturn turns Retrograde in Pisces so expect stalled progress in the outer world.

(I) Jupiter in Taurus Sextile Saturn in Pisces shows a resistance to progress in business and government. Taurus and Pisces natives should not take any external events personally.

(J) The Summer Solstice. Mercury Sextile Mars with a Leo Moon promotes heart inspiring confidence. An excellent time for Gemini, Virgo, Leo and Aries.

(K) This pair of Black Box Days mark challenging Transits. Mercury Square Neptune promotes confused communications and difficult past issues recurring. Tread lightly in the evening with conversations, especially with Aries and Libra.

(L) Two challenging Aspects may lead to technical problems, as well as social conflicts over money. Beware of deceptive practices. Mercury leaves 'short attention span' Gemini and enters cagey Cancer. Pay attention to making practical things work well in your home.

(M) This White Circle Day will benefit from determined work. If you stay focused, you will be able to accomplish a great deal. Excellent for Cancer and Scorpio.

(N) With the Sun Conjunct Mercury in Cancer, beware of too much mental stimulation. Spirit and ideas fuse during this Transit. Neptune turns Retrograde in Pisces, so dreams get put on hold for a little while. Go back and find some good ones that you forgot.

Currently many of the outer Planets are in the Signs, Capricorn, Aquarius and Pisces. So, as we move into the opposite Signs of Summer, Cancer, Leo and Virgo, those outer Planets will be Retrograde, contributing to our sense that the outer world and our personal life seem so different.

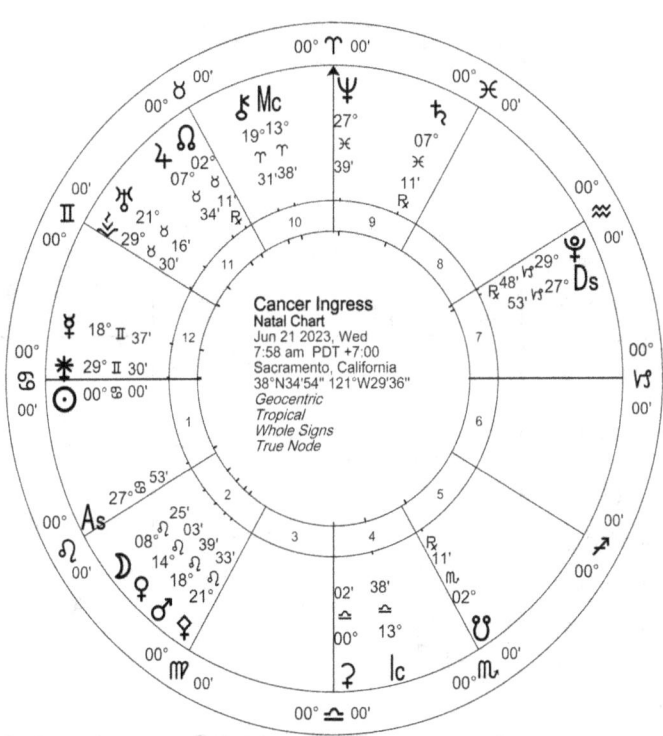

Signs

♈ Aries Begins
♉ Taurus Owns
♊ Gemini Engages
♋ Cancer Nurtures
♌ Leo Embraces
♍ Virgo Improves
♎ Libra Commits
♏ Scorpio Manages
♐ Sagittarius Views
♑ Capricorn Climbs
♒ Aquarius Herds
♓ Pisces Dreams

Planets

☉ Sun Spirit
☽ Moon Emotes
☿ Mercury Thinks
♀ Venus Feels
♂ Mars Acts
♃ Jupiter Expands
♄ Saturn Contracts
♅ Uranus Disrupts
♆ Neptune Envisions
♇ Pluto Unearths

Aspects

☌ Conjunct 0° Aligns
∥ Parallel 0° Equals
⚹ Sextile 60° Helps
□ Square 90° Works
△ Trine 120° Supports
☍ Opposition 180° Counters

Diverse Gemini says "I Engage"
Astro Notes:

JUNE 2023

Sunday	Monday	Tuesday
	♀ Enters ♋ 6:46am	
☽♐ **4** ☿☌♅ ♆ 8:23pm	**C** ☽♑ **5** ♃♄ ☉∥♀ ♀☌♇ 12:30am ———— 12:30am	♅☿♆ ☽♑ **6** 9:39pm ————
♇ Rx Enters ♑ 2:45am ☿ Enters ♊ 3:26am **F** ☽♈ **11** ♆♇☿♀ ☿∥♂ ♀□♃ 6:20am 6:19am - 6:20am	☽♈ **12** ♂ ☉⚹☽	♃ ♃ ☽♉ **13** 11:30am ♇ 11:26am - 11:30am
Father's Day ☽♋ **18** ♃♄ ☉□♆ 3:57am ———— 3:57am	Juneteenth **I** ☽♋ **19** ♅ ♃⚹♄	☽♌ **20** ♆ 3:03pm ♇ 2:43pm - 3:03pm
K ☽♎ **25** ♇ ☿□♆ 3:56pm 3:24pm - 3:56pm	1st Quarter ☽ 12:49am ☿ Enters ♋ 5:23pm **L** ☽♎ **26** ♆ ☉∥☽ ♂□♅	☽ **27** ♀☌♄

All calculations are Pacific Clock Time (PST & PDT)

Mercury☿ 16° Taurus♉ enters Gemini♊ on the 11th at 3:26am, enters Cancer♋ on the 26th at 5:23pm. Venus♀ 25° Cancer♋ enters Leo♌ on the 5th at 6:46am. Mars♂ 6° Leo♌. Jupiter♃ 3° Taurus♉. Saturn♄ 6° Pisces♓ turns Rx on the 17th at 10:27am at 7° Pisces♓. Uranus♅ 20° Taurus♉. Neptune♆ 27° Pisces♓ turns Rx on the 30th at 2:06pm at 27° Pisces♓. Pluto♇ Rx 00° Aquarius♒ enters Capricorn♑ on the 11th at 2:45am.

June 2023

Wednesday	Thursday	Friday	Saturday
	♄ ☽♏ 1 ♂☿	A ♆♀♇♇ ☽♐ 2 ♀△♆ 10:03pm ♅ 5:50pm - 10:03pm	Full ☽ 8:42pm 13° ♐ B ♂ ☽♐ 3 ☉☍☽ ♄
♇♇ ☽♒ 7 1:41am ♀♃♂ 1:41am	D ☽♒ 8 ☉△☽ ♅☿ 9:23pm	E ♃♄ ☽♓ 9 ☿⚹♆ 3:13am 3:13am	3rd Quarter ☽ 12:31pm ♄♅ ☽♓ 10 ☿∥♅ ☉□☽
Flag Day ♄♅ ☽♉ 14 ♂∥♅ ♀♂	G ♅♀☿♆♇ ☽♊ 15 ☿∥♀ ☿□♄ 6:45pm 6:36pm - 6:45pm	☿♀ ☽♊ 16 ☉∥☽ ♄	New ☽ 9:37pm 26° ♊ H ♂ ☉☌☽ ☽♊ 17 ☿⚹♀ ♄Rx ♆ 11:23pm
☉ Enters ♋ 7:58am J ☿♀ ☿⚹♂ ☽♌ 21 ☉∥☽ ♃ Summer Solstice	♂☿♀ ☽♌ 22 ♀∥♅ ♅ 10:00am	♂♃♃ ☉∥☿ ☽♍ 23 ☉⚹☽ 3:34am ♄ 3:34am	♅ ☽♍ 24
M ☿♄ ☉△♄ ☽♏ 28 ☉△☽ 1:55am ♇♃ 1:18am - 1:55am	Eid al Adha ☽♏ 29 ☿△♄ ♀♅♂	N ♆♇♇ ☽♐ 30 ☉☌☿ ♆Rx 7:59am ♄ 7:20am - 7:59am	

Add 1 Hour for Mountain Time (MT) Add 2 Hours for Central Time (CT) Add 3 Hours for Eastern Time (ET)

May into June 2023

Monday
Memorial Day

☽ ♎ **29** ♇♂
7:50am   ♆
2:45am - 7:50am

Tuesday

☽ ♎ **30** M ♆ ☉△☽

Wednesday

☽ ♏ **31** ♄
4:44pm ♀♇♃
7:53am - 4:44pm

Thursday

☽ ♏ **1** ♄
♂☿

May 29 thru June 4

Friday

A Ψ♀♇♇
☽♐ **2** ♀△Ψ
10:03pm ♅
5:50pm - 10:03pm

Saturday

Full ☽ 8:42pm 13° ♐

B ♂
☽♐ **3** ☉☌☽
♄

Sunday

☽♐ **4** ☿☌♅
Ψ
8:23pm --------

June 2023

Monday
♀ Enters ♌ 6:46am

C
☽♑ ♃♄ 5 ⊙∥♀
        ♀☍♇
12:30am

-------- 12:30am

Tuesday

♅☿♆
☽♑ 6

9:39pm --------

Wednesday

♇♇
☽♒ 7
1:41am ♀♃♂

-------- 1:41am

Thursday

D
☽♒ 8 ⊙△☽
♅☿
9:23pm --------

June 5 thru 11

Friday

E
☽♓ 9 ♃♄ ☿⚹♆
3:13am
3:13am

Saturday

3rd Quarter ☽ 12:31pm

☽♓ 10 ♄♅ ☿∥♅ ☉□☽

Sunday

♇ Rx Enters ♑ 2:45am
☿ Enters ♊ 3:26am

F ♆♇☿♆♀
☽♈ 11 ☿∥♂ ☿△♇
6:20am ♀□♃

6:19am - 6:20am

June 2023

Monday

☽ ♈ **12** ☉⚹☽

Tuesday

☽ ♉ **13** ♃ ♃
11:30am ♇
11:26am - 11:30am

Wednesday
Flag Day

☽ ♉ **14** ♄♅ ♂∥♅
♀♂

Thursday

G ♅♀☿♆♇
☽ ♊ **15** ☿∥♀
6:45pm ☿□♄
6:36pm - 6:45pm

June 12 thru 18

Friday

☽♊ **16** ☿♀ ☉∥☾ ♄

Saturday

New ☽ 9:37pm 26°♊

H ☽♊ **17** ♂ ☉☌☾ ☿⚹♀ ♄Rx ♆

11:23pm

Sunday
Father's Day

☽♋ **18** ♃♄ ☉□♆
3:57am

--------- 3:57am

June 2023

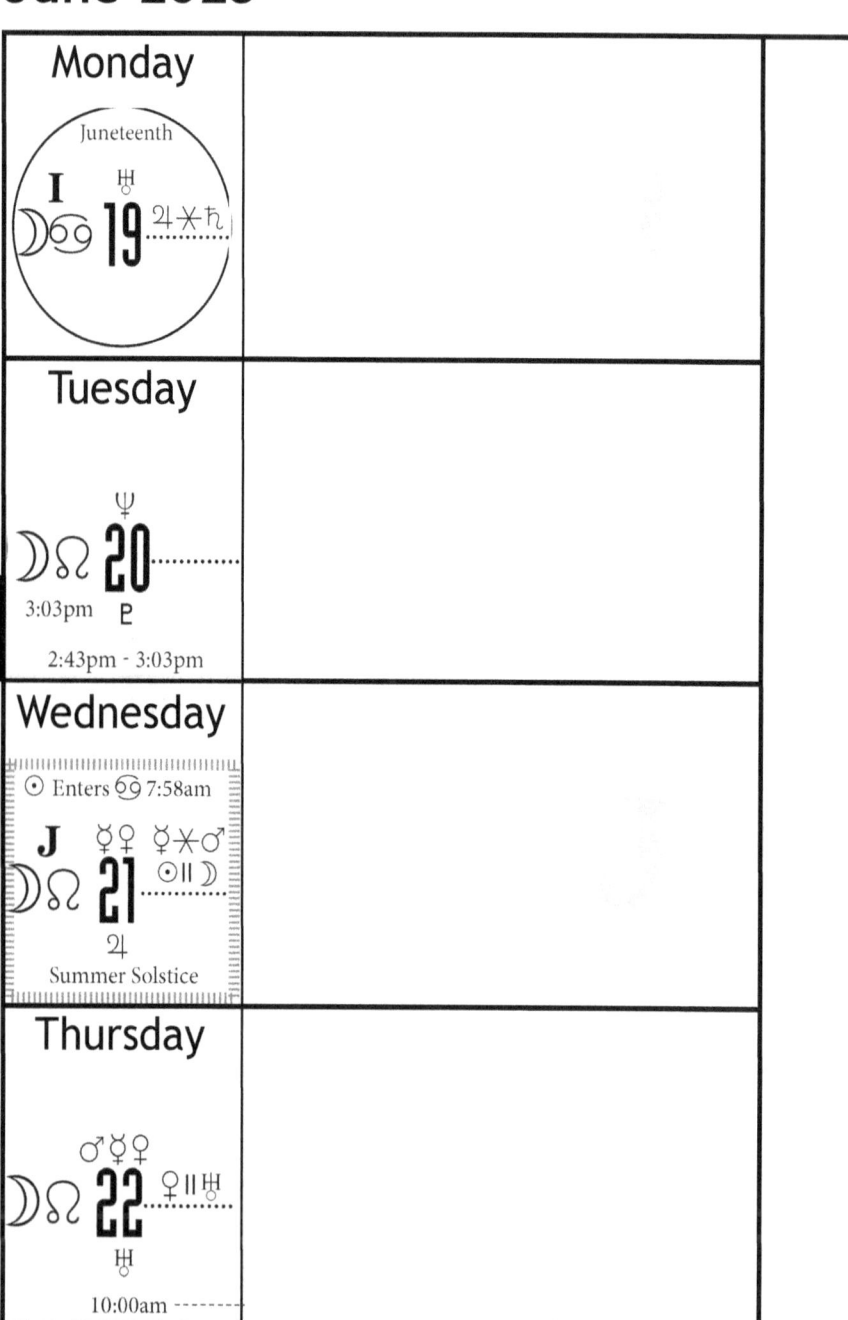

June 19 thru 25

Friday

☽♍ **23** ♂♃ ☉∥☿ ☉✶☽
3:34am ♄

-------- 3:34am

Saturday

☽♍ **24** ♅

Sunday

K P
☽♎ **25** ☿□♆
3:56pm ☿♆
3:24pm - 3:56pm

June into July 2023

Monday
1st Quarter ☽ 12:49am
☿ Enters ♋ 5:23pm

L ♆
☽︎ ♎ **26** ☉□☽
♂□♅

Tuesday

♀☌♄
☽︎ ♎ **27**

Wednesday

M ☿♄ ☉△♄
☽︎ ♏ **28** ☉△☽
1:55am ♇ ♃
1:18am - 1:55am

Thursday
Eid al Adha

☽︎ ♏ **29** ☿△♄
♀♅☌♂

June 26 thru July 2

Friday

N Ψ♇

☽♐ **30** ☉☌☿
7:59am ♄ ΨRx

7:20am - 7:59am

Saturday

A ♀ ☉✶♃
☽♐ **1** ☿✶♃

Sunday

♂♄
☽♑ **2** ♀□♅
10:19am Ψ

6:33am - 10:19am

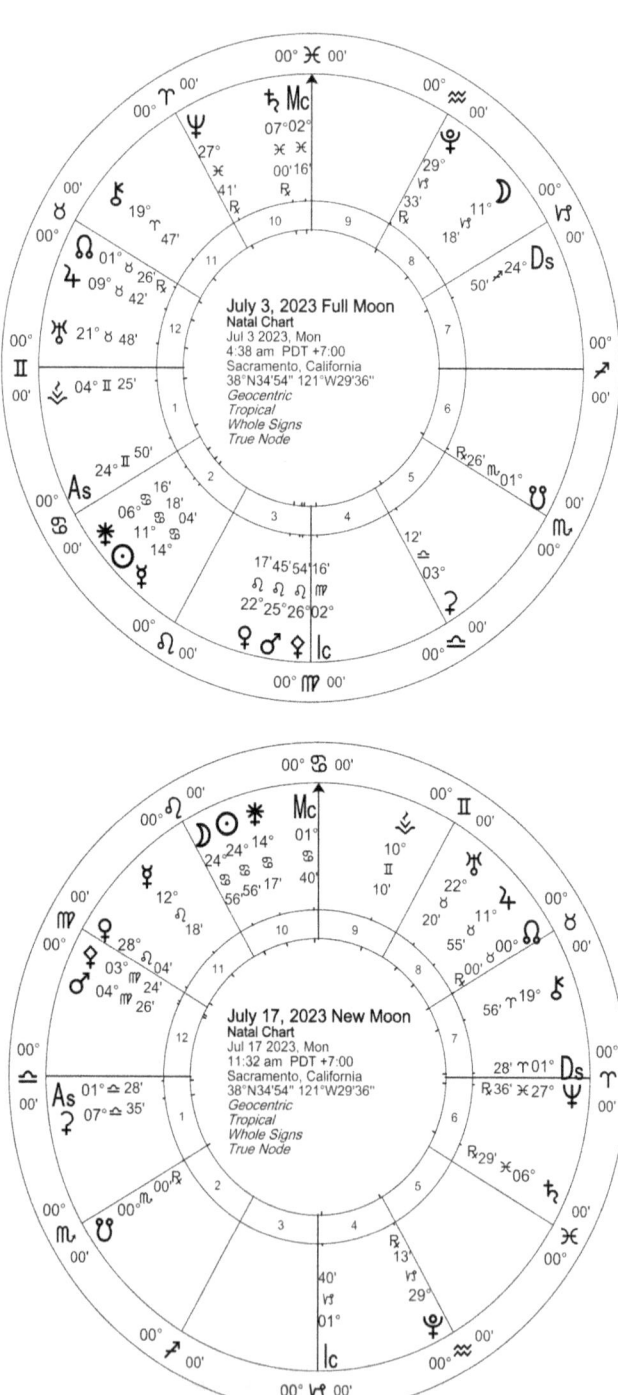

 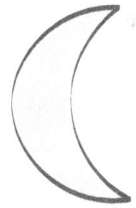 

July Forecasts
With Annotated Footnotes (A)
♋ Cancer the Crab to ♌ Leo the Lion

Mentally this is a fast-moving month with a quick Mercury, but socially more relaxed as Venus turns Retrograde in heart-based Leo. Mercury and Mars both change Signs on the 10th so expect to feel a shift in theme after that. The other event to watch is Mercury entering its Feminine Ruling Sign Virgo near the end of the month so let people help you. It's good for them and you!

(A) The White Circle Day's beneficial Aspects between the Sun and Mercury in Cancer and Jupiter in Pisces will be active on an emotional level, inspiring creativity. This is a suitable time to expand your ideas and your circle of influence. Generosity will tend to bring good returns. The Mutable Signs, Gemini, Virgo, Sagittarius and Pisces will resonate with this.

(B) The Cancer/Capricorn Full Moon highlights your emotional strength and perseverance. The Lunar Aspects from Jupiter and Uranus inspire you to go beyond your assumed limitations.

(C) The Cancer Sun Trine the Pisces Moon is a good time to push projects forward by taking advantage of available guidance and new tools. Great for the Water Signs.

(D) Expect turbulence today while Mars enters productive and detail focused Virgo, and Mercury enters drama-inclined Leo. Expect others to want your attention, encourage them to bring lunch, or at least coffee and snacks! Virgo, be careful not to physically overdo it, and watch out for bumping your head!

(E) A host of very stimulating Lunar Aspects with that Taurus Moon could bring interesting financial opportunities, especially for the Earth Signs, Taurus, Virgo and Capricorn.

(F) The Cancer New Moon supported by Uranus and Neptune contends with Mercury Square Jupiter, so great ideas may conflict with budgetary limitations. Good for Taurus, not so much for Leo.

(G) Later in the day after the Moon enters Virgo the need for detailed and craftsperson-like skills will be valued. The ability to dream big is increasing while the need to deal with the gritty details is keeping everything grounded. This could be a challenging time for Virgo and Pisces to find a common ground.

(H) The Sun enters Leo and the 'heart time' of the year. The Leo Sun Sextile the Libra Moon happens in the evening so plan some nice together time. Venus turns Retrograde in Leo, but Aphrodite does Retrograde better than most other Planets because it lets us internalize our sense of grace and harmony. In Leo it encourages us to restore our personal sense of style and glamour.

(I) The Black Box is all about that Mercury Square Uranus, while Neptune is Parallel the Moon in Libra. Both Planets are related to technology and communications but on different levels so watch out for problems with home appliances, local transportation and anyplace where electricity and people meet.

(J) With the Moon moving from Scorpio to Sagittarius amid a host of Lunar Aspects, and a Mercury Venus Conjunction in Leo, deep heart to heart talks could happen. Guide them in the best possible direction.

(K) The importance of the heart is called out as Mercury enters its Ruling Sign of Virgo, passing over the Star Regulus, the heart of the Constellation Leo. Meanwhile the Sun in Leo is Trine the powerful Moon in Sagittarius. You should feel the heart energy rising as general mental clarity and communications improve. Great for the Fire Signs.

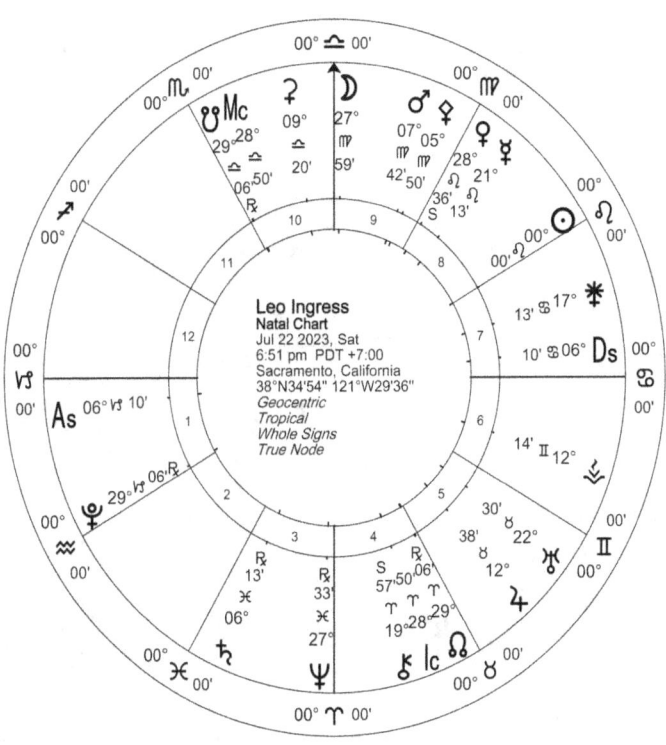

Signs

♈ Aries Begins
♉ Taurus Owns
♊ Gemini Engages
♋ Cancer Nurtures
♌ Leo Embraces
♍ Virgo Improves
♎ Libra Commits
♏ Scorpio Manages
♐ Sagittarius Views
♑ Capricorn Climbs
♒ Aquarius Herds
♓ Pisces Dreams

Planets

☉ Sun Spirit
☽ Moon Emotes
☿ Mercury Thinks
♀ Venus Feels
♂ Mars Acts
♃ Jupiter Expands
♄ Saturn Contracts
♅ Uranus Disrupts
♆ Neptune Envisions
♇ Pluto Unearths

Aspects

☌ Conjunct 0° Aligns
∥ Parallel 0° Equals
⚹ Sextile 60° Helps
□ Square 90° Works
△ Trine 120° Supports
☍ Opposition 180° Counters

Emotional Cancer says "I Feel"
Astro Notes:

JULY 2023

Sunday	Monday	Tuesday
☽♑ 30 ♄☌♃	☽♒ 31 ♅♆♇ ☉∥♅ 8:57pm 7:12pm - 8:57pm	
☽♑ 2 ♂♄ 10:19am ♀□♅ ♀♈ 6:33am - 10:19am	**B** ☽♑ 3 ♃♅ ☉☍☽ ☿ Full ☽ 4:38am 11° ♑ Supermoon	Independence Day ☽♒ 4 ♂∥♃ ♆♇ ♀∥♃ 10:29am ♀∥♂ 9:45am - 10:29am
☽♈ 9 ☿△♆ ☉□☽ 3rd Quarter ☽ 6:47pm	**D** ☽♉ 10 ☉∥☿ ♂ Enters ♍ 4:39am ♀ Enters ♌ 9:10pm ♀☌♂♀☌ ☿☌♇ 4:55pm ♇☿ 4:10pm - 4:55pm	☽♉ 11 ♃♄♃♅
☽♋ 16 ♃	**F** ☽♌ 17 ♅♆ ☉☌☽ ☿□♃ New ☽ 11:32am 24° ♋ 9:39pm ♇ 8:05pm - 9:39pm	☽♌ 18 ♀∥♅ ♃
I ☽♎ 23 ♆ ♀□♅	☽♎ 24 ☿∥♃	☽♏ 25 ♄♀♄ ☉□☽ 1st Quarter ☽ 3:06pm 9:55am ♇ 8:05am - 9:55am

All calculations are Pacific Clock Time (PST & PDT)

Mercury ☿ 9° Cancer ♋ enters Leo ♌ on the 10th at 9:10pm, enters Virgo ♍ on the 28th at 2:31pm. Venus ♀ 20° Leo ♌ turns Rx on the 22nd at 6:32pm at 28° Leo ♌. Mars ♂ 24° Leo ♌ enters Virgo ♍ on the 10th at 4:39am. Jupiter ♃ 9° Taurus ♉. Saturn ♄ Rx 7° Pisces ♓. Uranus ♅ 21° Taurus ♉. Neptune ♆ Rx 27° Pisces ♓. Pluto ♇ Rx 29° Capricorn ♑.

July 2023

Wednesday	Thursday	Friday	Saturday
			A ☽♐ **1** ☉✶♃ ☿✶♃
☽♒ **5** ♃♅	☽♓ **6** 10:32am ☿✶♅ ♀♂ 6:41am - 10:32am	**C** ☽♓ **7** ♃♄♅ ☉△☽ Bastille Day	☿♆♇ ☽♈ **8** 12:18pm 11:21am - 12:18pm
E ♅☿♆♇☉∥☽ ☽♉ **12** ☉✶♃ ♀ 11:10pm Muharram	☽♊ **13** 12:25am ♂♄ 12:25am	☽♊ **14** ☉✶♅	♀♂♄ ☽♋ **15** 10:13am ♆ 5:35am - 10:13am
☿ ☽♌ **19** ☉∥☽ ♅	**G** ☿♀♃♂ ☽♍ **20** ☉△♆ ♂♂♄ 10:12am ♄ 7:08am - 10:12am	♃♂♀ ☽♍ **21** ☉♂♇	☉ Enters ♌ 6:51pm **H** ☽♅♇ ☽♎ **22** ☉✶☽ ♀Rx 10:53pm ♆ 9:05am - 10:53am
♂ ☽♏ **26** ♃ Tisha B'Av	**J** ♆♇ ☽♐ **27** ☿♂♀ 5:23pm ♅♀☿ 3:35pm - 5:23pm	☿ Enters ♍ 2:31pm Delta Aquarid Meteors **K** ☽♐ **28** ☉△☽ ♄♂ Ashura	Delta Aquarid Meteors ♀☿ ☽♑ **29** 8:43pm ♆ 4:51pm - 8:43pm

Add 1 Hour for Mountain Time (MT) - Add 2 Hours for Central Time (CT) - Add 3 Hours for Eastern Time (ET)

July 2023

Monday

Full ☽ 4:38am 11° ♑
Supermoon

B ♃♅
☽♑ **3** ⋯⋯
☿ ☉☍☽

Tuesday

Independence Day

♂∥♃
Ψℙ ♀∥♃
☽≈ **4** ♀∥♂ ⋯⋯
10:29am

9:45am - 10:29am

Wednesday

ℙ
☽≈ **5** ⋯⋯
♃♅

Thursday

♄
☿⚹♅
☽♓ **6** ⋯⋯
10:32am ♀♂

6:41am - 10:32am

July 3 thru 9

Friday
C ♃♄♅
☽ ♓ **7** ☉△☽

Saturday
☿ΨΡΨ
☽ ♈ **8**
12:18pm

11:21am - 12:18pm

Sunday
3rd Quarter ☽ 6:47pm

☽ ♈ **9** ☿△Ψ
☉□☽

July 2023

Monday
♂ Enters ♍ 4:39am
☿ Enters ♌ 9:10pm
D ♀☌♂ ♀☌♂
☽ ♉ **10** ☉∥☿
4:55pm ☿☍♇
♇☿
4:10pm - 4:55pm

Tuesday
♃ ♄ ♃ ♅
☽ ♉ **11**

Wednesday
E ♅☿♆♇ ☉∥☽
☽ ♉ **12** ☉✶☽
♀
11:10pm

Thursday
☿
☽ ♊ **13**
12:25am ♂♄
-------- 12:25am

July 10 thru 16

Friday
Bastille Day

☽♊ **14** ☉✶♅

Saturday

☽♋ **15** ♀☌♄
10:13am ♆
5:35am - 10:13am

Sunday

☽♋ **16** ♃

July 2023

Monday

New ☽ 11:32am 24° ♋

F
☽ ♌ **17** ⛢ ♆
9:39pm   ☉☌☽
         ☿□♃
         ♇
8:05pm - 9:39pm

Tuesday

☽ ♌ **18** ☿∥⛢
      ♃

Wednesday
Muharram

           ☿
☽ ♌ **19** ☉∥☽
      ⛢

Thursday

     ☿♀♃♂
G
☽ ♍ **20** ☉△♆
10:12am   ♂☍♄
      ♄
7:08am - 10:12am

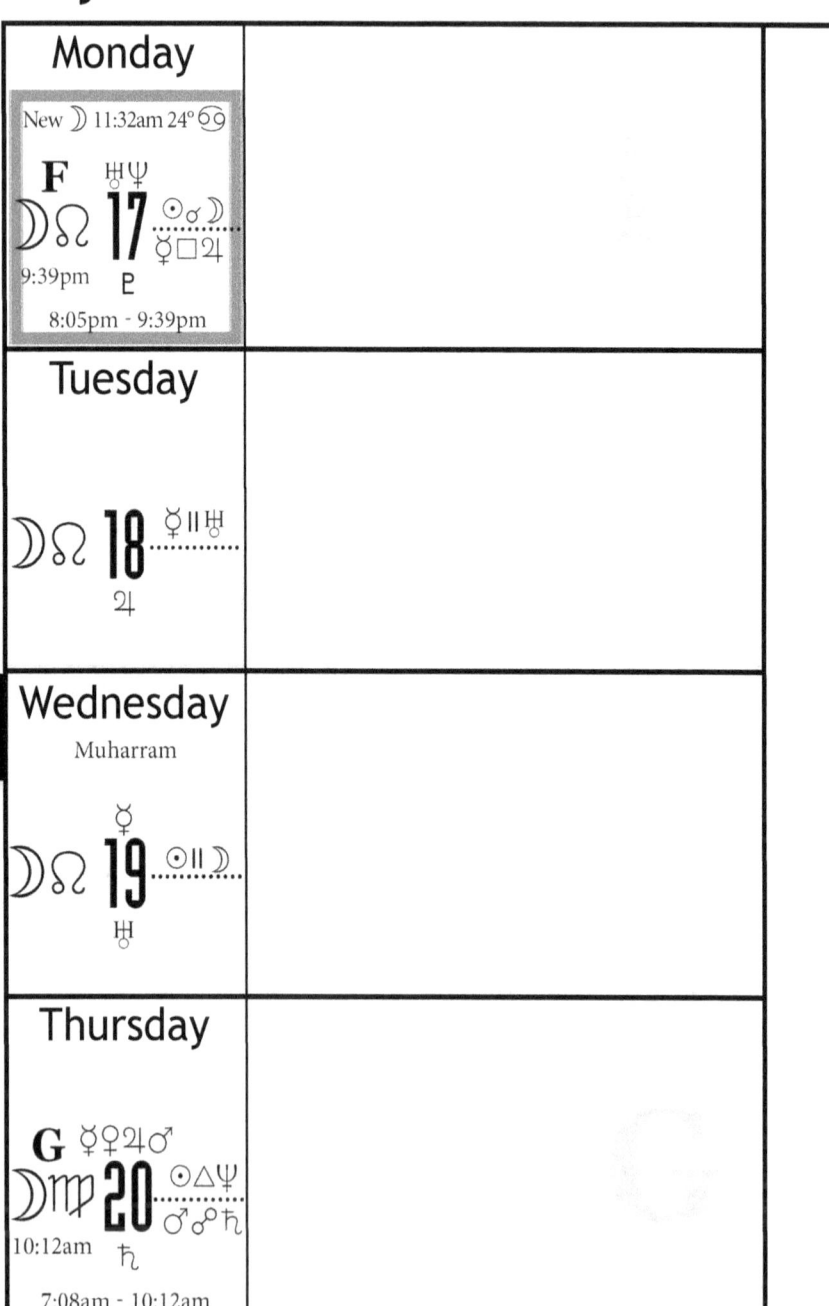

July 17 thru 23

Friday

☽♍ **21** ♃☌♀
☉☍♇

Saturday

☉ Enters ♌ 6:51pm

H ♅♇
☽♎ **22** ☉✶☽
♀Rx
10:53pm ♆
9:05pm - 10:53pm

Sunday

I ♆
☽♎ **23**
☿□♅

July into August 2023

Monday

☽ ♎ **24** ☿ ☿∥♃

Tuesday
1st Quarter ☽ 3:06pm

☽♏ **25** ♄♀♄ ☉□☽
9:55am ♇

8:05am - 9:55am

Wednesday

☽♏ **26** ♂
♃

Thursday
Tisha B'Av

☽♐ **27** J ♆♇♇ ☿♂♀
5:23pm ♅♀☿

3:35pm - 5:23pm

July 24 thru August 30

Friday

☿ Enters ♍ 2:31pm
Delta Aquarid Meteors

K

☽♐ **28** ☉△☽

♄♂

Ashura

Saturday

Delta Aquarid Meteors

♀☿

☽♑ **29**

8:43pm   ♆

4:51pm - 8:43pm

Sunday

♄♂♃

☽♑ **30**

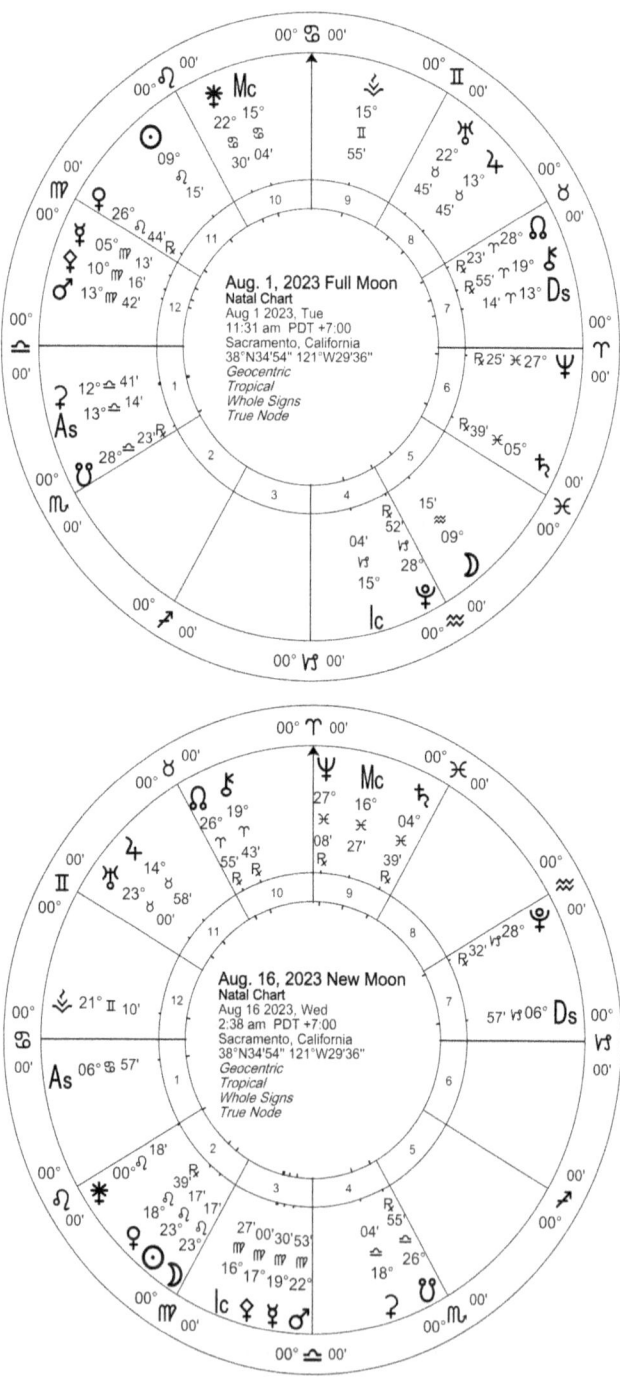

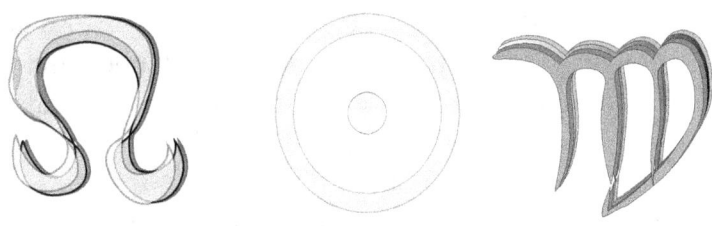

August Forecasts
With Annotated Footnotes (A)
♌ Leo the Lion to ♍ Virgo the Virgin

Astrologically, this is an uncomplicated month. Only Mars changes Sign, leaving productive Virgo for its Masculine Detriment Sign Libra so practical progress may lag. Meanwhile Mercury is slowing, preparing to turn Retrograde on the 23rd and on the 28th Uranus turns Retrograde too. As more outer Planets turn Retrograde external affairs stall. The inferior Conjunction of Venus and the Sun on the 13th is a big event.

The time when Venus stands directly between the Earth and the Sun is explored in myths from many cultures. They tell the story of a courageous woman who ventures into the depths of Hades to rescue her daughter, or her lover, depending on the culture. In various stories she is broken into parts by that journey, in other myths she must split her time between the heights and the depths. We see it as an analogy of the transformative journey of childbirth, when women travel on the verge of life and death to bring their beloved into the world of humans again. Being broken into parts? What does that mean? It was recently discovered that parts of a mother's brain material find their way into the brains of their children. If the brain is a communication device that transmits and receives on varied levels, then mothers have their children on speed dial. This Conjunction describes the deepest part of the journey.

(A) The month starts with a bang, thanks to a big Leo/Aquarius Full Moon, so those two Signs should pay attention because the spotlight is on you. Mars Trine Jupiter helps physical energy flow smoothly, but Mercury Opposed Saturn spurs conflicts between the generations.

(B) The Leo Sun Trine the Aries Moon is energizing to the Fire Signs making a harmonious day when things move along enthusiastically.

(C) The Sun in Leo Square Jupiter in Taurus brings up conflicts between what we want and what we do. A Void of Course Moon in Aries could stimulate disagreements, but the Taurus Moon in the afternoon encourages a mutually satisfying way forward.

(D) Lefthander's Day, the Perseid Meteors, a host of beneficial Lunar Aspects to a strong Cancer Moon while Venus makes an inferior Conjunction with the Sun. Venus will eventually reappear as the Morning Star. We discussed this spiritually profound day above. Leo prepare to do some soul searching.

(E) The Black Box for the Sun Square Uranus could show issues with technology or the environment coming to a head. Depending on location, this may mark the beginning of an extreme climatic event. The Fixed Signs may feel challenged.

(F) On this White Circle Day, Mars is Trine Uranus at the New Moon. Expand your use of technology to make physical tasks easier.

(G) Normally the last degrees of Leo are pleasant as the Sun Conjuncts the Star Regulus, but the Squares and Oppositions could cause polarization and disagreements about projected paths forward.

(H) The Sun moves into practical Virgo, and everyone feels like it's time to get back to work, but Mercury throws a wrench in the gears by turning Retrograde in later Virgo, Mercury's Feminine Ruling Sign. Expect a particularly difficult three-week Retrograde period ahead as communications and technology may tangle up and health issues recur.

(I) Take advantage of the Virgo Sun Trine the Capricorn Moon to get stalled projects moving. Great for the Earth Signs.

(J) Mars enters Libra, a position that encourages cooperation, personal balancing and grace over aggression. Libra watch out for physically overdoing it and for bumping your head.

(K) Uranus turns Retrograde further stalling progress in the outer world, so focus on the personal life instead.

(L) The second Full Super Moon of the Month between Virgo and Pisces puts those Signs in the spotlight along with Gemini and Sagittarius. Be flexible!

The Inferior Conjunction of Venus has often been celebrated in the arts including 'The Transit of Venus March' by famous composer John Philip Sousa, first performed in 1883 with Virgo Rising and Jupiter overhead.

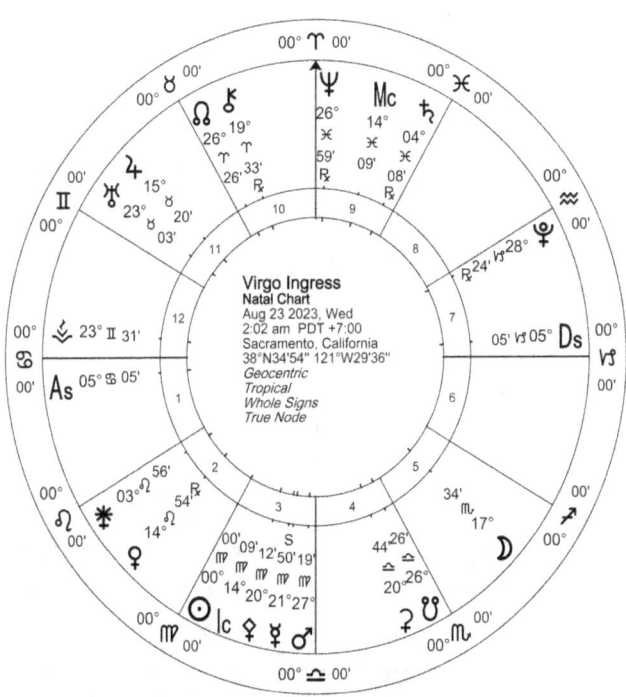

Signs

♈ Aries Begins
♉ Taurus Owns
♊ Gemini Engages
♋ Cancer Nurtures
♌ Leo Embraces
♍ Virgo Improves
♎ Libra Commits
♏ Scorpio Manages
♐ Sagittarius Views
♑ Capricorn Climbs
♒ Aquarius Herds
♓ Pisces Dreams

Planets

☉ Sun Spirit
☽ Moon Emotes
☿ Mercury Thinks
♀ Venus Feels
♂ Mars Acts
♃ Jupiter Expands
♄ Saturn Contracts
♅ Uranus Disrupts
♆ Neptune Envisions
♇ Pluto Unearths

Aspects

☌ Conjunct 0° Aligns
∥ Parallel 0° Equals
⚹ Sextile 60° Helps
□ Square 90° Works
△ Trine 120° Supports
☍ Opposition 180° Counters

Generous Leo says "I Will"

Astro Notes:

AUGUST 2023

Sunday	Monday	Tuesday
		Full ☽ 11:31am 9° ♒ Supermoon **A** ☽♒ 1 ♂△♃ ♀∥♂ ☉♂☽ ♃ ☿☌♄
C ♂☿♀ ☽♉ 6 ☉□♃ 11:24pm P 9:12pm - 11:24pm	♄♃☿☉∥☽ ☽♉ 7 ☿∥♂	3rd Quarter ☽ 3:28am ♃♅♂♅ ☽♉ 8 ☉□☽ ♀
Lefthander's Day Perseid Meteors **D** ☽☿♂♅ ☽♋ 13 ☉♂♀	☽♌ 14 3:36am P 12:46am - 3:36am	**E** ♀ ☽♌ 15 ☉□♅ ♃
♀ ☽♎ 20	♄ ☽♏ 21 ☉⚹☽ 4:21pm P 1:30pm - 4:21pm	**G** ♄ ☽♏ 22 ♀□♃ ♀♃ ♂☌♆
♂ Enters ♎ 6:19am **J** ♃☿♅ ☽♑ 27 ☉♂♄	**K** ♆♇☌♇ ☽♒ 28 ☉∥♀ 7:31am ♅Rx 4:48am - 7:31am	☽♒ 29 ♀♃♅ 8:04pm

All calculations are Pacific Clock Time (PST & PDT)

128

Mercury☿ 4° Virgo♍ turns Rx on the 23rd at 12:59pm at 21° Virgo♍. Venus♀Rx 26° Leo♌. Mars♂ 13° Virgo♍ enters Libra♎ on the 27th at 6:19am. Jupiter♃ 13° Taurus♉. Saturn♄Rx 5° Pisces♓. Uranus♅ 22° Taurus♉ turns Rx on the 28th at 7:38pm at 23° Taurus♉. Neptune♆Rx 27° Pisces♓. Pluto♇ Rx 28° Capricorn♑.

Wednesday	Thursday	Friday	Saturday
☽♓ **2** 8:05pm ♅♀ 2:15pm - 8:05pm	♄♄♃ ☽♓ **3** ☿♂	♅♆♇♆ ☽♈ **4** 8:19pm 6:20pm - 8:19pm	**B** ☉△☽ ☿‖♀ ☽♈ **5**
♆♇ ☽♊ **9** ☿△♃ ♀□♅ 6:04am ♄ 3:38am - 6:04am	♀ ☽♊ **10** ☉✶☽ ☿♂	☽♋ **11** ☉‖♃ 3:51pm ♆ 10:27am - 3:51pm	Perseid Meteors ♄♃ ☽♋ **12**
New ☽ 2:38am 23°♌ **F** ♃ ♂△♅ ☉☌☽ ☽♍ **16** 4:14pm ♅ 2:37am - 4:14pm	♃ ☽♍ **17** ☉‖☽ ♄	♀☿♅♂ ☽♍ **18** ♆	♇♂☿♆ ☽♎ **19** 4:53am 1:50am - 4:53am
☉ Enters ♍ 2:02am **H** ☿♆♂♇ ☽♏ **23** ☿Rx ♅ 10:10pm ----------	1st Quarter ☽ 2:57am ♇ ☽♐ **24** ♂△♇ ☉□☽ 1:07am ♄ ---------- 1:07am	♀ ☽♐ **25** ☿	**I** ♄ ☽♑ **26** ☉△☽ 6:05am ♆♂ 4:55am - 6:05am
Full ☽ 6:36pm 7° ♓ Supermoon/Blue Moon **L** ♄♄ ☽♓ **30** ☿‖♂ ☉☍☽ 6:56am Raksha Bandhan -------- 6:56am	♃♅ ☽♓ **31** ☿		

Add 1 Hour for Mountain Time (MT) - Add 2 Hours for Central Time (CT) - Add 3 Hours for Eastern Time (ET)

July to August 2023

Monday

☾ ≈ ♅♆♇ **31** ☉∥♅
8:57pm
7:12pm - 8:57pm

Tuesday

Full ☽ 11:31am 9° ≈
Supermoon

A ♇ ♂△♃
☾ ≈ **1** ♀∥♂
            ☉⚷☽
            ♃ ☿☍♄

Wednesday

☾ ♓ **2** ....
8:05pm ♅♀
2:15pm - 8:05pm

Thursday

           ♄♄♃
☾ ♓ **3** ....
      ☿♂

July 31 thru August 6

Friday

☽♈ **4** ♅♆♇
8:19pm

6:20pm - 8:19pm

Saturday

B
☽♈ **5** ☉△☽ ☿∥♀

Sunday

C ♂☿♀
☽♉ **6** ☉□♃
11:24pm ♇

9:12pm - 11:24pm

August 2023

Monday

☽ ♉ **7** ♄ ♃ ☿ ☉∥☽
          ☿∥♂

Tuesday

3rd Quarter ☽ 3:28am

☽ ♉ **8** ♃♆︎♂♅
       ♀   ☉□☽

Wednesday

☽ ♊ **9** ♆ ♇
6:04am   ☿△♃
       ♄   ♀□♅

3:38am - 6:04am

Thursday

☽ ♊ **10** ♀ ☉✶☽
       ☿♂

August 7 thru 13

Friday

☽ ♋ **11** ☉∥♃
3:51pm ♆
10:27am - 3:51pm

Saturday
Perseid Meteors

♄ ♃
☽ ♋ **12**

Sunday
Lefthander's Day
Perseid Meteors

D ☿ ♂ ♅ ♆
☽ ♋ **13** ☉☌♀

August 2023

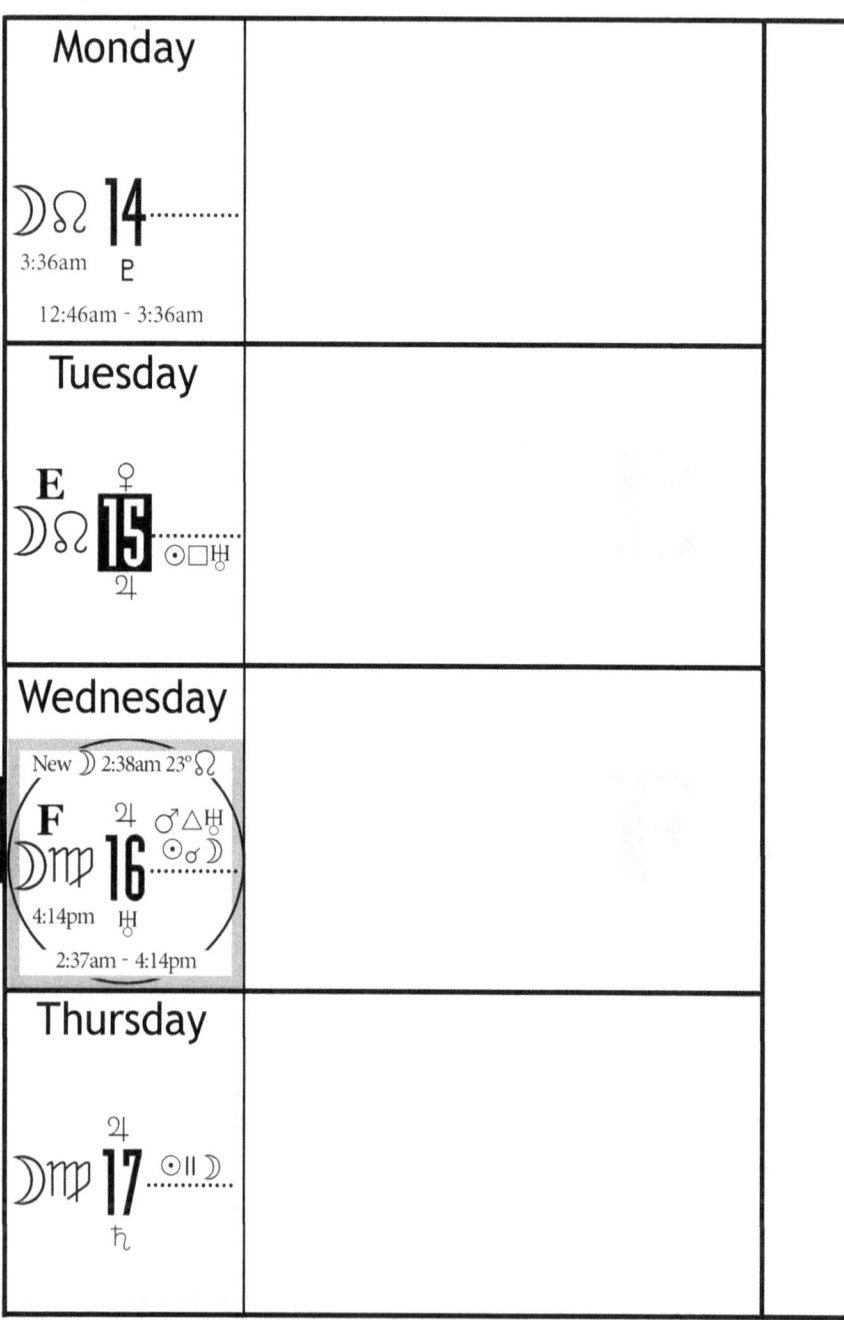

August 14 thru 20

Friday

☽♍ 18 ♀☿♅♂ ♆

Saturday

☽♎ 19 ♇♂☿♆
4:53am

1:50am - 4:53am

Sunday

☽♎ 20 ♀

August 2023

Monday

☽♏ 21 ☉✶☽
♄
4:21pm
♇
1:30pm - 4:21pm

Tuesday

G
☽♏ 22 ♄
♀♃ ♀□♃
       ♂☍♆

Wednesday

☉ Enters ♍ 2:02am
H ☿♆♂♇
☽♏ 23 ☿Rx
♅
10:10pm

Thursday

1st Quarter ☽ 2:57am

☽♐ 24 ♇
      ♂△♇
      ☉□☽
1:07am
♄
-------- 1:07am

August 21 thru 27

Friday
☿
☽♐ **25**
☿

Saturday
I ♄
☽♑ **26** ☉△☽
6:05am ♆☌♂
4:55am - 6:05am

Sunday
♂ Enters ♎ 6:19am
J ♃☿♅
☽♑ **27**
☉☍♄

137

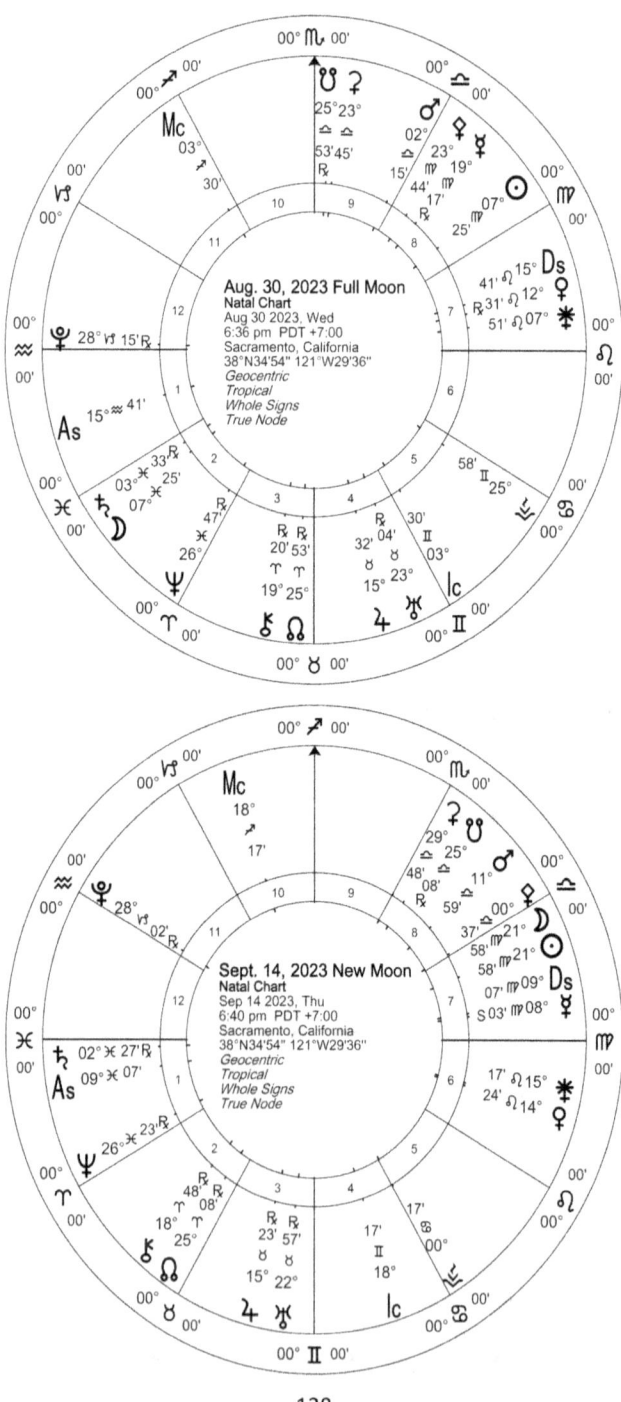

September Forecasts
With Annotated Footnotes (A)
♍ Virgo the Virgin to ♎ Libra the Scales

September is unique because no Planets change Sign. Now directions, that's another issue! Mercury spends the first half of the month Retrograde in Virgo turning Direct on the 15th right after the New Moon so the glitches will fade. Meanwhile Venus turns Direct in Leo on the 3rd so the social life will pick up. Finally, Jupiter turns Retrograde on the 4th in the middle of Taurus, so now all the Planets from there out to Pluto are Retrograde. While the personal life is moving along well, the BIG world may be a bit stalled. This month is the calm before the storm because there are a pair of Eclipses coming up in October.

(A) Venus, still in heart-based Leo, turns Direct focusing its attention on the people around us and encouraging generosity and drama. Leo finally gets some help!

(B) Jupiter in Taurus turns Retrograde, and that's the only thing that stops this from being a White Circle Day because business meetings and planning sessions can be very productive.

(C) The Sun and Retrograde Mercury are Conjunct in Virgo, so Gemini, Virgo and Aquarius watch out for overloaded nervous systems.

(D) The first of two White Circle Days with a strong Cancer Moon happens while the Sun and Jupiter are Trine, supporting practical and profitable projects, helped by supportive Lunar Aspects from Saturn and Mercury.

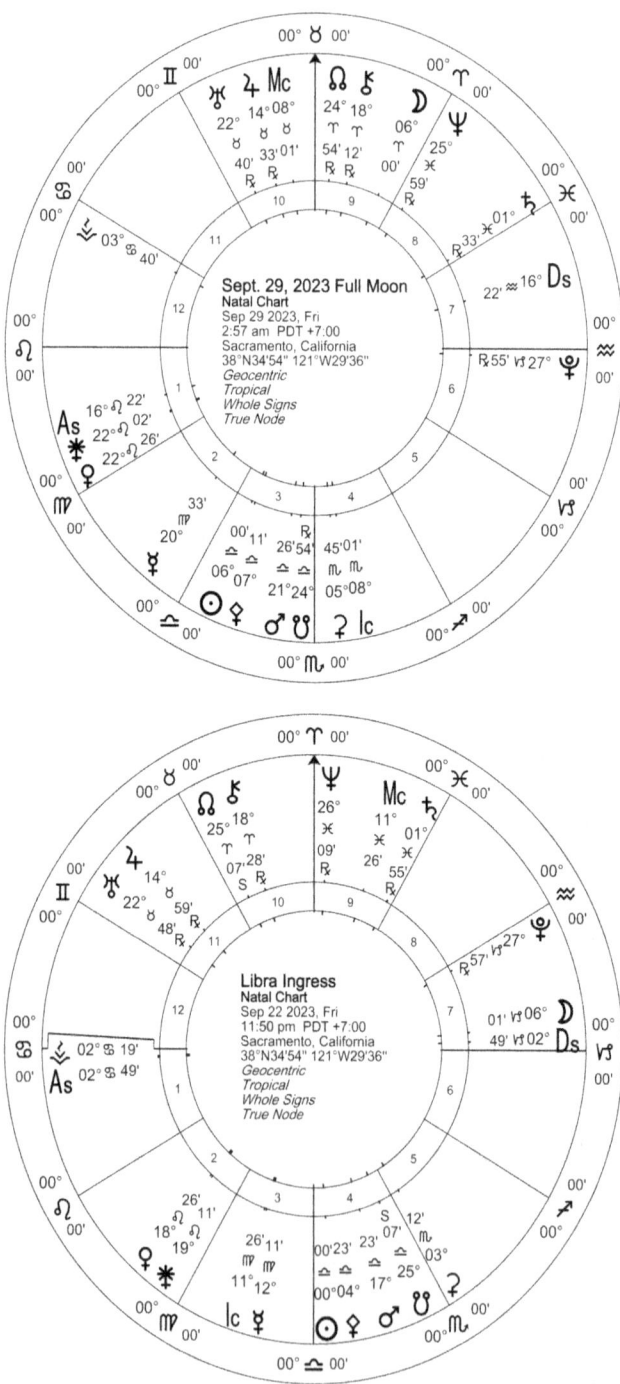

(E) Yesterday's beneficial Aspects are augmented by the Sun Sextile Moon and both Jupiter and Uranus lending a helping hand. Whatever you start during this weekend will have the wind at its back. Especially good for Taurus, Cancer, Virgo and Pisces.

(F) This Virgo New Moon's White Circle Day owes its recommendation to the following day's Transits which it incorporates. A good time to start a health-promoting diet or exercise program.

(G) Mercury turns Direct smoothing out communications, technology and travel, while the Sun in Virgo Trine Uranus in Taurus expands the importance of seeking innovative solutions to health, environmental and climatic issues. Gemini, Virgo and Aquarius rejoice!

(H) This Venus in Leo Square Jupiter in Taurus could result in family arguments over money, made worse by incorrect information. Aries and Libra beware.

(I) The Sun Opposed Neptune could stimulate floods or chemical spills, or just inspire you to shout at the TV over the stupidity often displayed there. Pisces take care.

(J) This White Circle Day is not very personal, focused instead on the outer world, although Capricorn may find that things run more smoothly.

(K) The Sun entering Libra, the Autumnal Equinox, happens at the First Quarter Moon. The next three months are an excellent period for participating in projects in cooperation with others that will help your reputation in your community.

(L) This Black Box Day, rather than being the province of any challenging Aspects, is instead uncomfortably distracted due to a long Void of Course Moon in Aquarius that starts early and ends late. Having Mars and Saturn help during the day is a mixed blessing, as problematic as the challenges from Venus and Uranus. Don't be too ambitious about the day and make a list of what you want to accomplish.

(M) The Libra/Aries Full Moon is complicated by Venus in Leo Square Uranus in Taurus, so watch out for pride butting heads with stubbornness, resulting in arguments and negotiations. Instead, go out to a nice lunch.

Signs

♈ Aries Begins
♉ Taurus Owns
♊ Gemini Engages
♋ Cancer Nurtures
♌ Leo Embraces
♍ Virgo Improves
♎ Libra Commits
♏ Scorpio Manages
♐ Sagittarius Views
♑ Capricorn Climbs
♒ Aquarius Herds
♓ Pisces Dreams

Planets

☉ Sun Spirit
☽ Moon Emotes
☿ Mercury Thinks
♀ Venus Feels
♂ Mars Acts
♃ Jupiter Expands
♄ Saturn Contracts
♅ Uranus Disrupts
♆ Neptune Envisions
♇ Pluto Unearths

Aspects

☌ Conjunct 0° Aligns
∥ Parallel 0° Equals
⚹ Sextile 60° Helps
□ Square 90° Works
△ Trine 120° Supports
☍ Opposition 180° Counters

Precise Virgo says "I Analyze"

Astro Notes:

SEPTEMBER 2023

Sunday	Monday	Tuesday
A ♀♄♃ ☽♉ **3** ♀'D' 7:59am ♇ 4:56am - 7:59am	Labor Day **B** ☿♃♅☉△☽ ☽♉ **4** ☿△♃ ♀ ♃Rx	♅♆♇ ☽♊ **5** 1:06pm ♄ 9:45am - 1:06pm
Grandparents Day ♆ ☽♌ **10** 9:35am ♇ 5:47am - 9:35am	☽♌ **11** ♂♀ ♃	♃ ☽♍ **12** 10:17pm ♅ 8:05am - 10:17pm
Constitution Day ♄ ☽♏ **17** 9:57pm ♇ 6:06pm - 9:57pm	Ganesh Chaturthi ♄☿ ☽♏ **18**	**I** ☽♏ **19** ☉♀♆ ♃♀♅
♅♆♇ ☽♒ **24** ☉△☽ 4:29pm 1:05pm - 4:29pm	Yom Kippur ♇ ☽♒ **25** ☿△♃ ♃	**L** ♂♄ ☽♓ **26** 5:17pm ♀♅ 5:38am - 5:17pm

All calculations are Pacific Clock Time (PST & PDT)

Mercury☿ Rx 18° Virgo♍ turns Direct on the 15th at 1:20pm at 8° Virgo♍. Venus♀ Rx 12° Leo♌ turns Direct on the 3rd at 6:19pm at 12° Leo♌. Mars♂ 3° Libra♎.
Jupiter♃ 15° Taurus♉ turns Rx on the 4th at 7:10am at 15° Taurus♉. Saturn♄ Rx 3° Pisces♓. Uranus♅ Rx 23° Taurus♉. Neptune♆ Rx 26° Pisces♓. Pluto♇ Rx 28° Capricorn♑.

Wednesday	Thursday	Friday	Saturday
		♆♇♆☿ ☽♈ 1 6:24am ♂ 3:35am - 6:24am	♀ ☽♈ 2 ☉∥☽
3rd Quarter ☽ 3:20pm C ♂♀ ☽♊ 6 ☉☌☿ ☉□☽ ☿	☽♋ 7 9:59pm ♆ 3:21pm - 9:59pm	D ♄☿ ♂∥♆ ☉△♃ ☽♋ 8 ♂	California Admission Day E ♃♅ ☉∥☿ ☉⚹☽ ☽♋ 9
☿♀ ☽♍ 13 ♄	New ☽ 6:40pm 21°♍ F ♃☿♅ ☽♍ 14 ☉☌☽	G ♇ ☉△♅ ☿'D' ☉∥☽ ☽♎ 15 10:44am ♆ 6:49am - 10:44am	Rosh Hashanah H♆♂♂♀ ☽♎ 16 ♀□♃
J ♆♇♇ ☉△♇ ☉⚹☽ ☽♐ 20 7:05am ♄ 3:21am - 7:05am	♂♀ ☽♐ 21 ☿	☉ Enters ♎ 11:50pm 1st Quarter ☽ 12:31pm K ♄ Fall Equinox ☽♑ 22 ☉□☽ 1:20pm ♆ 12:31pm - 1:20pm	☿♃ ☽♑ 23 ♂
The Prophet's Birthday ♄♃♂ ☽♓ 27 ☿	♅♆♇♆ ☽♈ 28 ☉∥☽ 5:17pm 1:57pm - 5:17pm	Full ☽ 2:57am 6° ♈ Supermoon M ☿ ☽♈ 29 ☉☍☽ ♀□♅	Sukkot First Day ♀♀♄ ☿△♅ ☉∥♆ ☽♉ 30 6:17pm ♂♇ 2:49pm - 6:17pm

Add 1 Hour for Mountain Time (MT) - Add 2 Hours for Central Time (CT) - Add 3 Hours for Eastern Time (ET)

August into September 2023

Monday

K ♆♇♂♇
☽♒ **28** ☉∥♀
     ♅Rx
7:31am

4:48am - 7:31am

Tuesday

☽♒ **29**
♀♃♅
8:04pm --------

Wednesday

Full ☽ 6:36pm 7° ♓
Supermoon/Blue Moon
L ♄♄
☽♓ **30** ☿∥♂
     ☉☍☽
6:56am
Raksha Bandhan
-------- 6:56am

Thursday

♃♅
☽♓ **31** ....
☿

August 28 thru September 3

Friday

☽♈ 1 ΨPΨ☿
6:24am ♂
3:35am - 6:24am

Saturday

☽♈ 2 ♀
⊙∥☽

Sunday

A
☽♉ 3 ♀♄♃
7:59am ♀'D'
♇
4:56am - 7:59am

September 2023

Monday
Labor Day

☽ ♉ **B** 4 ☿♃♅ ☉△☽
☿△♃
♃Rx
♀

Tuesday

☽♊ 5 ♅ѰP
♄
1:06pm
9:45am - 1:06pm

Wednesday
3rd Quarter ☽ 3:20pm

☽♊ **C** 6 ♂♀
☉☌☿
☉□☽
☿

Thursday

☽♋ 7 Ѱ
9:59pm
3:21pm - 9:59pm

September 4 thru 10

Friday

D ♋ ♄☿ ♂∥♆
8 ☉△♃
♂

Saturday
California Admission Day

E ♋ ♃♅ ☉∥☿
9 ☉✶☽

Sunday
Grandparents Day

☽ ♌ ♆
10
9:35am ♇

5:47am - 9:35am

September 2023

Monday
☽ ♌ **11** ♂♀ ♃

Tuesday
☽ ♍ **12** ♃ ♅
10:17pm
8:05am - 10:17pm

Wednesday
☽ ♍ **13** ☿♀ ♄

Thursday
New ☽ 6:40pm 21°♍
F ☽ ♍ **14** ♃☿♅ ☉☌☽

September 11 thru 17

Friday

☉△♅
☿'D'
☉⚹☽

☽♎ **G** ♇ **15**
10:44am ♆

6:49am - 10:44am

Saturday

Rosh Hashanah

H♆♂♂♀
☽♎ **16**
♀□♃

Sunday

Constitution Day

♄
☽♏ **17**
9:57pm ♇

6:06pm - 9:57pm

September 2023

Monday

Ganesh Chaturthi

☽♏ 18 ♄☿

Tuesday

I

☽♏ 19 ☉☌♆
♃♀♅

Wednesday

J ♆♇ ☉△♇
☽♐ 20 ☉⚹☽
7:05am ♄
3:21am - 7:05am

Thursday

♂♀
☽♐ 21
☿

September 18 thru 24

Friday

☉ Enters ♎ 11:50pm
1st Quarter ☽ 12:31pm

K ♄ Fall Equinox
☽ ♑ **22** ☉□☽
1:20pm ♆

12:31pm - 1:20pm

Saturday

☿ ♃
☽ ♑ **23**
♂

Sunday

♅ ♆ ♇
☽ ♒ **24** ☉△☽
4:29pm

1:05pm - 4:29pm

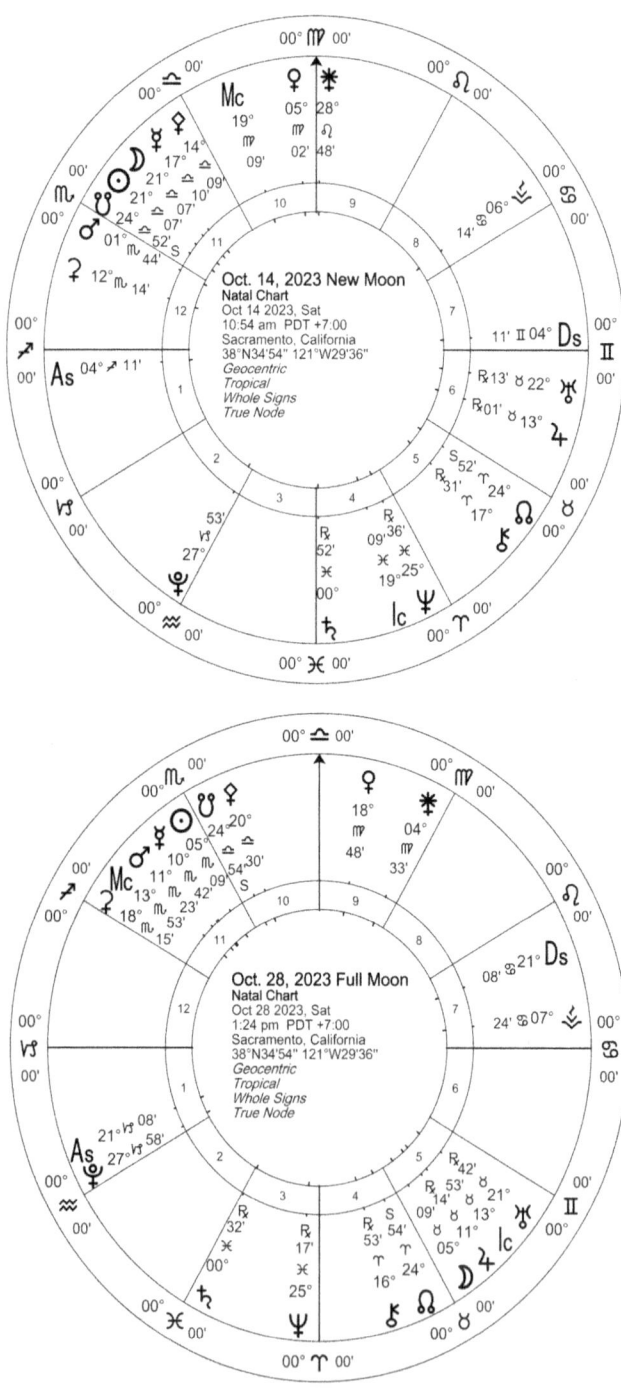

October Forecasts
With Annotated Footnotes (A)
♎ Libra the Scales to ♏ Scorpio the Scorpion

Mercury moves quickly through three Signs. Venus leaves Leo for Virgo, appearing as the Morning Star at maximum visibility on October 23rd, when she becomes the Warrior Goddess. Mars enters powerful, feminine Scorpio. This affects the personal life as energy shifts to the feminine.

(A) This an easy day to get things done, although with Saturn Square the Moon don't getting bogged down with worries. Good for the Air Signs.

(B) Mercury leaves analytical Virgo for contemplative Libra. Decisions will take longer but make negotiations an opportunity for brainstorming.

(C) Venus, after being in Leo since June, enters service centered Virgo. Issues of love and beauty make way for practicalities, responsibilities and health. Virgo prepare to be popular.

(D) Pluto turns Direct. As the outer Planets gradually turn Direct expect to feel the sea change. This is the final direction change for Pluto before entering Aquarius in January 2024, after which it will dip back into Capricorn before returning to Aquarius.

(E) Mars enters Scorpio, the Sign of womanly power and the traditional Feminine Ruler of Mars. After Pluto's discovery, unnamed astrologers, unfamiliar with Sacred Geometry, erroneously assigned Scorpio, the archetype of Martial, feminine reactive power to a nebulous rock at the farthest reaches of the Solar System. Mars in Scorpio is one of the Planet's strongest positions so that Sign will feel the power.

(F) This is a mild Day especially good for Capricorn and Aquarius and business matters although the Eclipse the next day could screw things up.

(G) Big Event! This New Moon in Libra is an Annular Eclipse, which means that there will be a ring of the Sun visible around the Moon. It is being called the Great American Eclipse because its path begins off the coast of Washington State, sweeping down through the west, across Texas into the Gulf of Mexico (the midpoint), curving south through Central America, Colombia and east through Brazil reaching the Atlantic at the eastern most point of South America. This event happens two degrees away from the feminine Star Spica in the Constellation Virgo. Every Planet is in feminine Signs except the Sun, Moon and Mercury in Libra, a Venus Ruled Sign. It foretells dramatic events in the Americas over the next year related to law, partnerships, marriage, women's rights and climate change. In the short term, the time between the New Moon and the second Eclipse at the Full Moon on the 28th will be emotionally complex. Use this time to find the places in your life that feel out of balance, and work on improving their harmony and gracefulness. Libra and Aries do soul searching.

(H) With the Sun Conjunct Mercury watch out for mental over-stimulation. Beware, Gemini, Libra and Aquarius.

(I) Quick Mercury enters determined Scorpio at the Quarter Moon with Venus Trine Jupiter; people will want to quickly get to the point. Good for Mercury Ruled Signs, Gemini, Virgo and Aquarius.

(J) The Sun enters Scorpio, a powerfully feminine time of the year when people are willing to dive into the deeper issues. Good for the Water Signs.

(K) There are so many Lunar and Planetary Aspects today that it may get chaotic with too many distractions.

(L) The Full Moon Partial Eclipse in early Taurus/Scorpio can promote anger and rage so be careful and shield yourself. With three major Oppositions going on there will be a heightened sense of polarity.
Patience, this will pass! The Fixed Signs should take it slow.

(M) With Venus Trine Uranus, design meets innovation and it's a perfect time to say Boo. Happy Halloween!

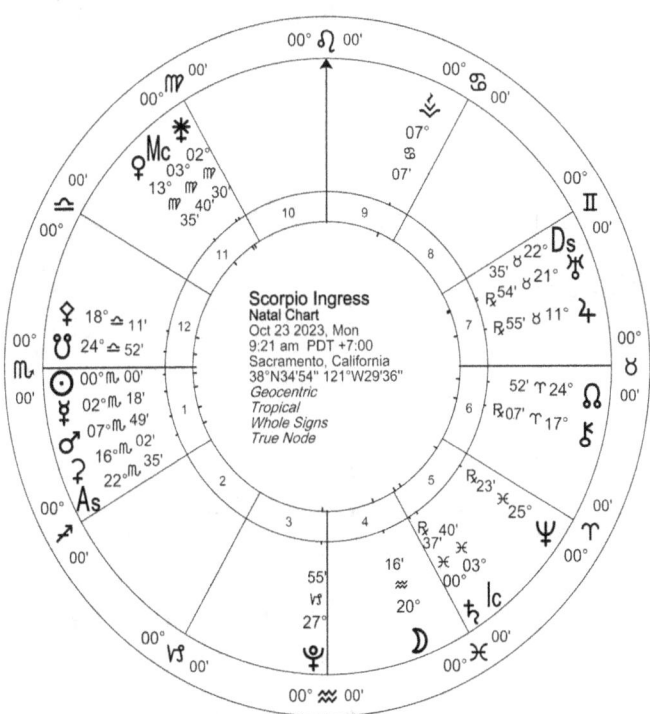

Signs

♈ Aries Begins
♉ Taurus Owns
♊ Gemini Engages
♋ Cancer Nurtures
♌ Leo Embraces
♍ Virgo Improves
♎ Libra Commits
♏ Scorpio Manages
♐ Sagittarius Views
♑ Capricorn Climbs
♒ Aquarius Herds
♓ Pisces Dreams

Planets

☉ Sun Spirit
☽ Moon Emotes
☿ Mercury Thinks
♀ Venus Feels
♂ Mars Acts
♃ Jupiter Expands
♄ Saturn Contracts
♅ Uranus Disrupts
♆ Neptune Envisions
♇ Pluto Unearths

Aspects

☌ Conjunct 0° Aligns
‖ Parallel 0° Equals
⚹ Sextile 60° Helps
□ Square 90° Works
△ Trine 120° Supports
☍ Opposition 180° Counters

Fair Libra says "I Balance"

OCTOBER 2023

Sunday	Monday	Tuesday
	♃♅ ☽♊ **2** 10:02pm ♀ 6:19pm - 10:02pm	☉△☽ A ☽♊ **3** ☿△♇ ♄
♀ Enters ♍ 6:10pm Simchat Torah C ☽♌ **8** ☿ ♂□♇ ♃	Indigenous Peoples Day ☽♌ **9** ☉⚹☽ ♅ ☿☌♄	D ♂♀♃ ☿‖♆ ☽♍ **10** ♇ 'D' 5:01am ♄ 2:36am - 5:01am
Navratri ♂♄☽♂♀ ☽♏ **15** 4:03am ♇ 12:00am - 4:03am	☽♏ **16** ♃♅	♆♇ ☽♐ **17** 12:36pm ♄ 8:43am - 12:36pm
Orionid Meteors ♇ ☿△♄ ☽♒ **22** ☉‖☿ ♂♃	☉ Enters ♏ 9:21am Dussehra J ☽♒ **23** ♅ 12:04pm -----	♄♂☿♄☿☌♃ K ☽♓ **24** ☿‖♄ ☉‖☽ 1:32am ☉△♄ ----- 1:32am
♅♀♅♆ ☽♉ **29** ☿☌♂ ☿♂	☽♊ **30** ♇ 8:07am ♄ 4:35am - 8:07am	Halloween M ☽♊ **31** ♀△♅

All calculations are Pacific Clock Time (PST & PDT)

156

Mercury ☿ 23° Virgo ♍ enters Libra ♎ on the 4th at 5:08pm, enters Scorpio ♏ on the 21st at 11:48pm. Venus ♀ 23° Leo ♌ enters Virgo ♍ on the 8th at 6:10pm. Mars ♂ 22° Libra ♎ enters Scorpio ♏ on the 11th at 9:03pm. Jupiter ♃ Rx 14° Taurus ♉. Saturn ♄ Rx 1° Pisces ♓. Uranus ♅ Rx 22° Taurus ♉. Neptune ♆ Rx 25° Pisces ♓. Pluto ♇ Rx 27° Capricorn ♑ turns Direct on the 10th at 6:09pm 27° Capricorn ♑.

October 2023

Wednesday	Thursday	Friday	Saturday
☿ Enters ♎ 5:08pm **B** ☐♂♀ ☽♊ **4** ♆ 11:34pm	♄ ☽♋ **5** 5:31am ♉ ---- 5:31am	3rd Quarter ☽ 6:47am Sukkot Ends ♃ ☽♋ **6** ⊙□☽	Draconid Meteors Shemini Atzeret ♅♆ ☽♌ **7** 4:24pm ♂♇ 12:11pm - 4:24pm
♂ Enters ♏ 9:03pm **E** ♃♀ ☽♍ **11**	♅♇ ☽♎ **12** 5:21pm ♆ 1:10pm - 5:21pm	**F** ♆☿ ☽♎ **13** ☿△♄	New ☽ 10:54am 21°♎ Annular ⊙ Eclipse **G** ☿ ⊙∥☽ ☽♌ **14** ⊙♂☽
			1st Quarter ☽ 8:29pm ☿ Enters ♏ 11:48pm
☽♐ **18** ♂∥♄ ♀	**H** ☿♄ ⊙♂☿ ☽♑ **19** ⊙⚹☽ 6:54pm ♆ 12:01pm - 6:54pm	♂♀♃ ☽♑ **20** ☿□♇	**I** ♅♆♇ ☽♒ **21** ♀△♃ 11:05pm ☿ ⊙□☽ Orionid Meteors 11:00pm - 11:05pm
			Full ☽ 1:24pm 5°♉ Partial ☽ Eclipse
♅♆♇ ☽♓ **25** ♀ 11:38pm	☽♈ **26** 3:01am ---- 3:01am	♀ ☽♈ **27** ⊙∥♄	**L** ♄♃ ☿∥♂ ☽♉ **28** ♂♂♃ 4:43am ⊙♂☽ ♇ ☿♂♃ 1:19am - 4:43am

Add 1 Hour for Mountain Time (MT) - Add 2 Hours for Central Time (CT) - Add 3 Hours for Eastern Time (ET)

September into October 2023

Monday
Yom Kippur

☽ ≈ **25** ⚝△♃ ♇ ☿△♃
♃

Tuesday

L ♂♄
☽ ♓ **26**
5:17pm ♀♅

5:38am - 5:17pm

Wednesday
The Prophet's Birthday

♄♃♂
☽ ♓ **27**
☿

Thursday

♅ ♆ ♇
☽ ♈ **28** ☉☋☽
5:17pm

1:57pm - 5:17pm

September 25 thru October 1

Friday

Full ☽ 2:57am 6° ♈
Supermoon
M ☿
☽♈ **29** ☉☍☽
♀□♅

Saturday

Sukkot First Day

♀♀♄ ☿△♅
☽♉ **30** ☉∥♆
6:17pm ♂♇

2:49pm - 6:17pm

Sunday

♃ ♃♅
☽♉ **1**

October 2023

Monday

☽ ♊ **2** ⛢ ♆ ♇
10:02pm   ☿ ☍ ♆
             ♀
6:19pm - 10:02pm

Tuesday

A
☽ ♊ **3** ☉ △ ☽
            ☿ △ ♇
            ♄

Wednesday

☿ Enters ♎ 5:08pm

B ♂ ♀
☽ ♊ **4**
       ♆
11:34pm

Thursday

☽ ♋ **5** ♄
5:31am   ☿
------ 5:31am

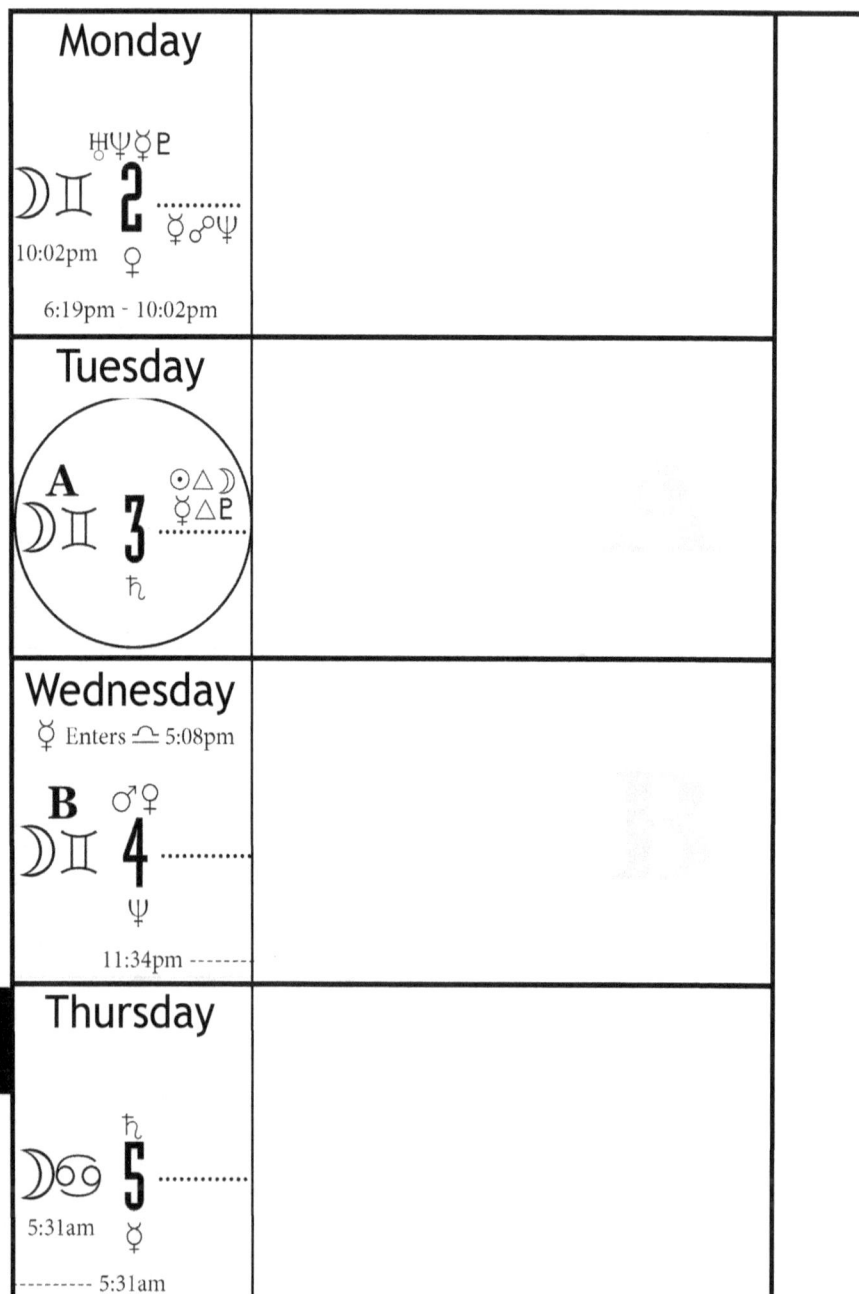

October 2 thru 8

Friday
3rd Quarter ☽ 6:47am
Sukkot Ends

♃
☽♋ **6** ⊙□☽

Saturday
Draconid Meteors
Shemini Atzeret

♅♆
☽♌ **7**

4:24pm ♂♇

12:11pm - 4:24pm

Sunday
♀ Enters ♍ 6:10pm
Simchat Torah

C ☿
☽♌ **8** ♂□♇
♃

October 2023

Monday
Indigenous Peoples Day

☽♌ **9** ☉✶☽
⛢ ☿☍♄

Tuesday

D ♂♀♃ ☿∥♆
☽♍ **10** ♇'D'
5:01am ♄

2:36am - 5:01am

Wednesday
♂ Enters ♏ 9:03pm

E ♃♀
☽♍ **11**

Thursday

⛢♇
☽♎ **12**
5:21pm ♆

1:10pm - 5:21pm

October 9 thru 15

Friday
F ☾♎ 13 ♆☿ ☿△♄

Saturday
New ☾ 10:54am 21°♎
Annular ☉ Eclipse
G ☿ ☉∥☽
☾♎ 14 ☉☌☽

Sunday
Navratri

♂♄ ♄♂♀
☾♏ 15
4:03am ♇
12:00am - 4:03am

October 2023

Monday

☽ ♏ **16**
♃ ♅

Tuesday

♆ ♇
☽ ♐ **17**
12:36pm ♄
8:43am - 12:36pm

Wednesday

☽ ♐ **18** ♂ ∥ ♄
♀

Thursday

H ☿ ♄ ☉ ☌ ☿
☽ ♑ **19** ☉ ✶ ☽
6:54pm ♆
12:01pm - 6:54pm

October 16 thru 22

Friday

☽ ♑ **20** ♂♀♃
☿□♇

Saturday

1st Quarter ☽ 8:29pm
☿ Enters ♏ 11:48pm

☽ ≈ **21** ♅♆♇
♀△♃
☉□♇
11:05pm ☿ ☉□☽
Orionid Meteors
11:00pm - 11:05pm

Sunday

Orionid Meteors

☽ ≈ **22** ♇ ☿△♄
☉‖☿
♂♃

October 2023

Monday
☉ Enters ♏ 9:21am
Dussehra

J
☽ ≈ **23**
♅
12:04pm

Tuesday

♄ ♂ ☿ ♄ ☌ ♂ ♃
K   ☿ ∥ ♄
☽ ♓ **24**   ☉ ∥ ☽
1:32am   ☉ △ ☽
                 ☉ △ ♄

-------- 1:32am

Wednesday

♅ ♆ ♇
☽ ♓ **25**
♀
11:38pm

Thursday

☽ ♈ **26**
3:01am

-------- 3:01am

166

October 23 thru 29

Friday

☽ ♈ **27** ☉∥♄ ♀

Saturday

Full ☽ 1:24pm 5° ♉
Partial ☽ Eclipse

L ♄ ♃ ☿∥♂
☽ ♉ **28** ♂ ⚹ ♃
4:43am ☉ ⚹ ☽
♇ ☿ ⚹ ♃

1:19am - 4:43am

Sunday

♅ ♀ ♅ ♆
☽ ♉ **29** ☿ ☌ ♂
☿ ♂

167

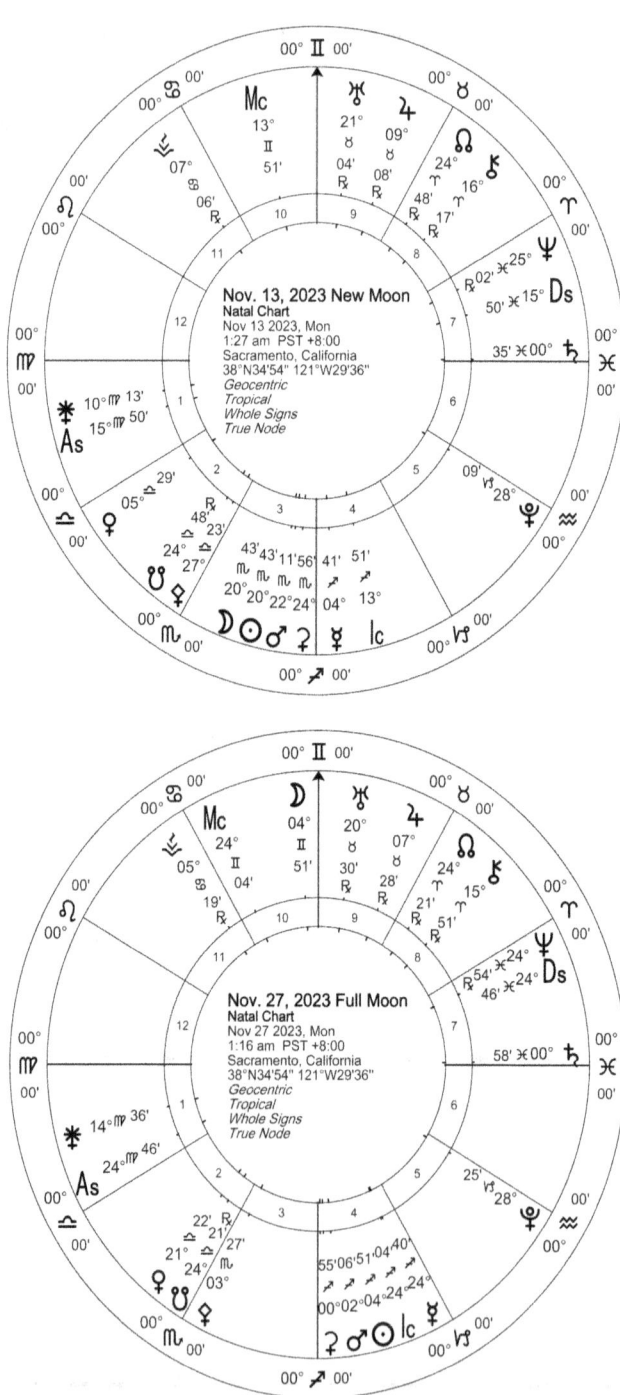

November Forecasts
With Annotated Footnotes (A)
♏ Scorpio the Scorpion to ♐ Sagittarius the Archer

After the tumult of October this November is calm in comparison. Mercury, Venus and Mars, now all Direct, change Signs so personal relationships shift. Then Saturn, after moving Retrograde all the way to Zero degrees Pisces, turns Direct on the 4th, so large projects will progress again. The month is balanced between easy and challenging transits.

(A) This is a good time to move things along but expect resistance from those who may prefer the status quo. Very good for the Water Signs.

(B) Saturn turns Direct, so stalled group projects see forward movement.

(C) Don't plan to accomplish much today. It would lead to conflicts that are especially hard for Leo and Aquarius.

(D) This day should flow smoothly with a beneficial Lunar Aspect from Jupiter to the hard-working Virgo Moon and a pair of Trines connecting Mercury and Venus to the Outer Planets.

(E) Venus entering its Social Dynamic (Ruling Masculine) Sign of Libra will help connect people together for the rest of the month. A profusion of beneficial Lunar Aspects to the industrious Virgo Moon can make this a very productive, and yet pleasantly social day.

(F) Mercury enters Sagittarius, so conversations may get a little scattered all month, but they will be fun and upbeat.

(G) This New Moon in Scorpio Opposes Uranus in Taurus. Expect to hear about conflicts between commerce and the environment. Multiple Lunar Aspects make this a very social day with excessive demands on your time. Challenging for Leo and Aquarius, but productive for Virgo and Pisces.

(H) Beneficial Aspects between the Sun, Mars, Neptune and Moon move events forward smoothly allowing ideas to become reality more easily. The drive to get things done may suffer from too many distractions, so stay off social media. Good for practical Taurus, Virgo and Capricorn.

(I) The Sun enters Sagittarius on a pleasant Sun Trine Moon Day. These Lunar Aspects happen early so it is a less social day than it might appear. Sagittarius, like Thanksgiving, represents abundance and sharing. It follows Scorpio when the herds are thinned and meat is preserved for Winter.

Expansive, lucky Sagittarius is Jupiter's Dynamic Social Ruler. Pisces is the Responsive Personal Ruler. After the discovery of Neptune unnamed Astrologers, unaware of the underlying Geometry, assigned Pisces to Neptune. This decision has colored the way that we see Neptune by ascribing to it the qualities of Pisces, while removing those qualities from Jupiter. We think that was a mistake!

To understand the power of Jupiter in Pisces, consider the events that happened in the first half of 2022 when Jupiter was flying through Pisces while the suffering of Ukraine was broadcast to the world.

(J) With Mars leaving intense Scorpio for optimistic Sagittarius, maybe Black Friday will be the biggest of the past few years. Get out into the world, see friends, expand your territory and find ways to help your neighbors and community. Sagittarius natives, be aware that your energy will go up during this Transit so be careful about physically overdoing it and acting impulsively. This is good for the Fire Signs!

(K) This Full Moon creates a challenging T-Square tying together the Sun, Moon, Mercury and Neptune. The four Mutable Signs, Sagittarius, Gemini, Virgo and Pisces, will feel the pressure the most. To make this day work will take a great deal of effort, but focus on people over things or ideas and you will have more success.

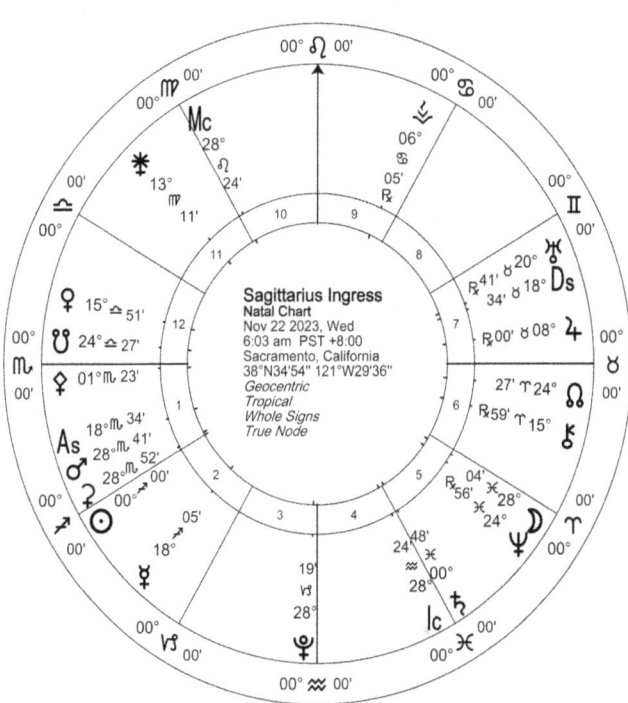

Signs

♈ Aries Begins
♉ Taurus Owns
♊ Gemini Engages
♋ Cancer Nurtures
♌ Leo Embraces
♍ Virgo Improves
♎ Libra Commits
♏ Scorpio Manages
♐ Sagittarius Views
♑ Capricorn Climbs
♒ Aquarius Herds
♓ Pisces Dreams

Planets

☉ Sun Spirit
☽ Moon Emotes
☿ Mercury Thinks
♀ Venus Feels
♂ Mars Acts
♃ Jupiter Expands
♄ Saturn Contracts
♅ Uranus Disrupts
♆ Neptune Envisions
♇ Pluto Unearths

Aspects

☌ Conjunct 0° Aligns
‖ Parallel 0° Equals
✶ Sextile 60° Helps
□ Square 90° Works
△ Trine 120° Supports
☍ Opposition 180° Counters

Passionate Scorpio says "I Empower"

Astro Notes:

NOVEMBER 2023

Sunday	Monday	Tuesday
3rd Quarter ☽ 1:36am Taurid Meteors Daylight Time Ends ☽ ♌ **5** C ☉□☿ ♂♅☿ 11:25pm Diwali	D ♃ ☿△♆ ☽♍ **6** ♀△♇ 11:38am ♄ ----- 11:38am New ☽ 1:27am 20°♏	Election Day ♃ ☽♍ **7** ☉✶☽
☽♏ **12** ☉‖ ♃	G ♂♆♀♇ ☽♐ **13** ☉☌☽ 6:22pm ♅♄ 3:03pm - 6:22pm	☿♀ ☽♐ **14** ☿‖♇
♀☿♂ ☉‖♂ ☽♒ **19** ☉‖☽ ♅	1st Quarter ☽ 2:49am ♄♄♃ ☽♓ **20** ☉✶♇ ☉□♆ 6:28am ♂ 2:49am - 6:28am	♅ ☽♓ **21** ♂✶♇ ☿
♅♆♇ ☽♊ **26** 4:39pm ♄♂ 1:51pm - 4:39pm	Full ☽ 1:16am 4° ♊ K ☽♊ **27** ☉☍☽ ☿♊♀ Cyber Monday	♀ ☽♋ **28** ♀ 10:53pm ♆ 5:02pm - 10:53pm

All calculations are Pacific Clock Time (PST & PDT)

172

Mercury☿ 16° Scorpio♏ enters Sagittarius♐ on the 9th at 10:24pm. Venus♀ 22° Virgo♍ enters Libra♎ on the 8th at 1:30am. Mars♂ 13° Scorpio♏ enters Sagittarius♐ on the 24th at 2:14am. Jupiter♃ Rx 10° Taurus♉. Saturn♄ Rx 0° Pisces♓ turns Direct on the 4th at 12:02am. Uranus♅Rx 21° Taurus♉. Neptune♆Rx 25° Pisces♓. Pluto♇° 28° Capricorn♑.

Wednesday	Thursday	Friday	Saturday
♄ ☽♋ **1** .... 2:30pm ♀♆ 5:36am - 2:30pm	A ♃♂ ☽♋ **2** ☉△☽ ☉☍♃	☿♅♀♆ ☽♋ **3** ♀☍♆ ♇ 8:27pm ----------	Taurid Meteors B ☽♌ **4** ♄'D' ☿☍♅ 12:20am ♃ ---------- 12:20am
♀ Enters ♎ 1:30am E ♂♅♇☿ ☽♍ **8** ☿⚹♇ ♆ 8:54pm ----------	☿ Enters ♐ 10:24pm F ♀♀♆ ☽♎ **9** .... 12:07am ---------- 12:07am	Veterans Day Holiday ☽♎ **10** ☿□♄	Veterans Day ♄♄ ☽♏ **11** ♂☍♅ 10:38am ♇ 7:05am - 10:38am
☽♑ **15** ☿⚹♀ 11:41pm ♆ 2:56pm - 11:41pm	♄♃ ☽♑ **16** .... ♀	Leonid Meteors H ♅♆♂ ☽♑ **17** ☉☌♂ ☉⚹☽ ☉△♆ ♂△♆	Leonid Meteors ♇☿♇ ☽♒ **18** ♀∥♆ 3:27am ♃ 12:27am - 3:27am
☉ Enters ♐ 6:03am I ♀♆♆♇♂ ☽♈ **22** ☉△☽ 9:19am 7:09am - 9:19am	Thanksgiving Day ☿ ☽♈ **23** ☉□♄ ♀	♂ Enters ♐ 2:14am Black Friday J ♄♃ ☽♉ **24** .... 12:28pm ♇ 9:40am - 12:28pm	♃♅ ☽♉ **25** ♂□♄
♄♃ ☽♋ **29**	♅♆ ☽♋ **30**		

Add 1 Hour for Mountain Time (MT) - Add 2 Hours for Central Time (CT) - Add 3 Hours for Eastern Time (ET)

October into November 2023

Monday

☽ ♊ **30** ᴾ
8:07am ♄
4:35am - 8:07am

Tuesday

Halloween

M
☽ ♊ **31** ♀△♅

Wednesday

☽ ♋ **1** ♄
2:30pm ♀♆
5:36am - 2:30pm

Thursday

A
☽ ♋ **2** ♃♂ ☉△☽
☉☍♃

October 30 thru November 5

Friday

☿♅♀♆
))♋ **3** ⋯ ♀☌♆
♇

8:27pm ----------

Saturday
Taurid Meteors

B
))♌ **4** ⋯ ♄'D'
12:20am ♃ ☿☌♅

-------- 12:20am

Sunday
3rd Quarter)) 1:36am
Taurid Meteors
Daylight Time Ends

))♌ **5** ⋯ **C**
    ☉□))
♂♅☿

11:25pm --------

November 2023

Monday
D
☽♍ 6 ♃ ☿△♆
              ♀△♇
11:38am ♄
------ 11:38am

Tuesday
Election Day

☽♍ 7 ♃ ☉✶☽

Wednesday
♀ Enters ♎ 1:30am

E
☽♍ 8 ♂♅♇☿
        ☿✶♇
       ♆
8:54pm ------

Thursday
☿ Enters ♐ 10:24pm

F ♀♀♆
☽♎ 9 ....
12:07am

------ 12:07am

November 6 thru 12

Friday
Veterans Day Holiday

☽︎ ♎︎ **10** ☿☐♄

Saturday
Veterans Day

♄ ♄
☽︎ ♏︎ **11** ♂︎ ☌ ♅
10:38am ♇
7:05am - 10:38am

Sunday
Diwali

♂︎
☽︎ ♏︎ **12** ☉ ⚻ ☽︎
♃

November 2023

Monday

New ☽ 1:27am 20°♏

G ♂♆♇☿♀
☽♐ **13** ☉♂☽
6:22pm ♅♄ ☉♂♅
3:03pm - 6:22pm

Tuesday

☽♐ **14** ☿♀ ☿∥♇

Wednesday

☽♑ **15** ☿✶♀
11:41pm ♆
2:56pm - 11:41pm

Thursday

☽♑ **16** ♄♃ ♀

November 13 thru 19

Friday

Leonid Meteors

H ♅Ψ♂ ☉☌♂
)♑ 17 ☉⚹☽
        ☉△Ψ
        ♂△Ψ

Saturday

Leonid Meteors

♇☿♇
)♒ 18 ♀∥Ψ
3:27am ♃

12:27am - 3:27am

Sunday

♀☿♂ ☉∥♂
)♒ 19 ☉∥☽
♅

November 2023

Monday
1st Quarter ☽ 2:49am

☽ ♓ **20** ♄♄♃ ☉✶♇
6:28am   ☉□☽
♂
2:49am - 6:28am

Tuesday

☽ ♓ **21** ♅ ♂✶♇
♀

Wednesday
☉ Enters ♐ 6:03am

I ♀♆♇♂
☽ ♈ **22** ☉△☽
9:19am
7:09am - 9:19am

Thursday
Thanksgiving Day

☽ ♈ **23** ☿
☉□♄
♀

180

November 20 thru 26

Friday

♂ Enters ♐ 2:14am
Black Friday

J ♄♃
☽♉ **24**
12:28pm ♇

9:40am - 12:28pm

Saturday

♃♅
☽♉ **25**
♂□♄

Sunday

♅♆♇
☽♊ **26**
4:39pm ♄♂

1:51pm - 4:39pm

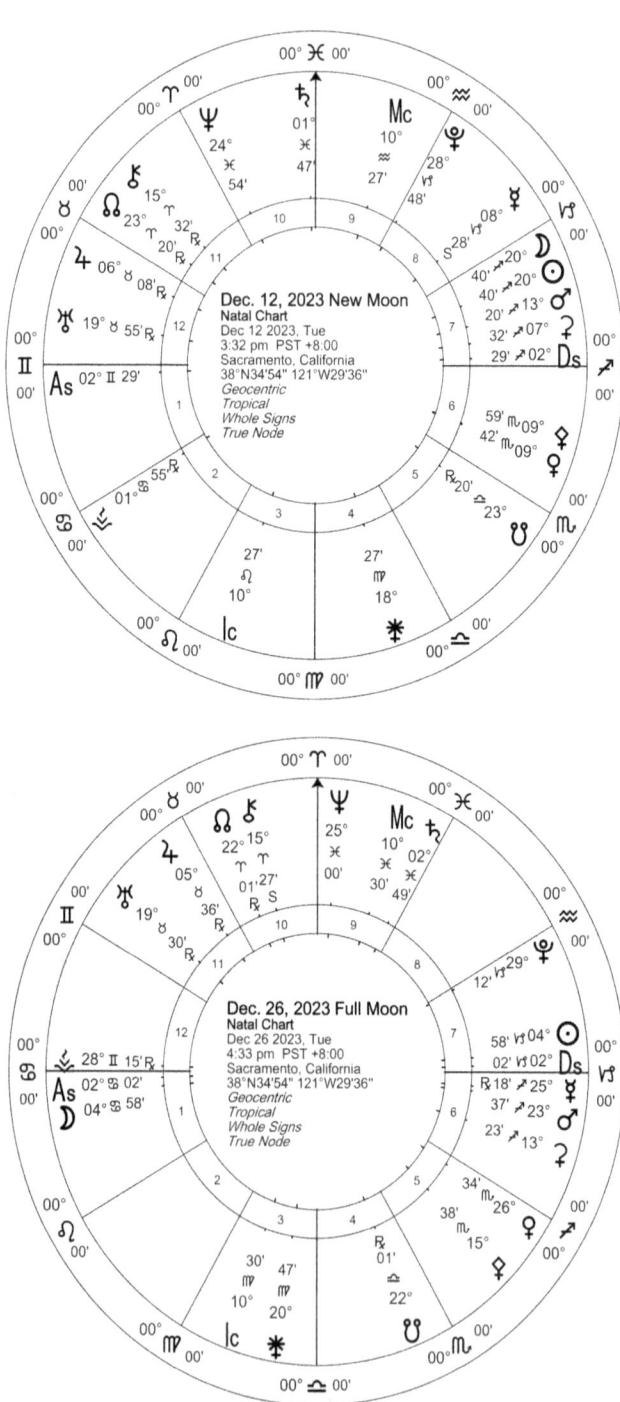

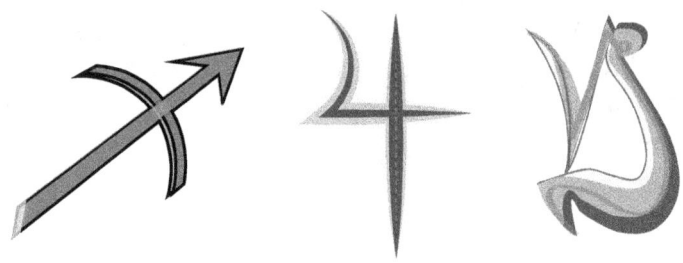

December Forecasts
With Annotated Footnotes (A)
♐ **Sagittarius the Archer to** ♑ **Capricorn the Sea Goat**

This is a month with mixed messages as a slowing Mercury enters Capricorn before turning Retrograde on the 12th and backing into Sagittarius the next week. So, get your holiday shopping done early! A quickly moving Venus, visiting three Signs this month, rushes social matters along as well as commerce. Affairs of the heart may turn serious. Jupiter and Neptune turn Direct, in harmony with Saturn, so the economy and the political world will have the juice to move ahead again. Beware because Jupiter will eventually Conjunct Uranus in Taurus in April of 2024, most likely disrupting both climate and economies. The Sun enters Capricorn on the 21st at the Winter Solstice followed by a series of supportive Aspects between the big Planets through the end of the year, describing a time when cooperation and progress are being promoted.

(A) Mercury moves from philosophical Sagittarius into ambitious Capricorn. This is very good for the Earth Signs, Taurus, Virgo and Capricorn, but Mercury is slowing so work fast.

(B) A very helpful Sun Trine Moon, complemented by a business minded Mercury Sextile Saturn, could help you accomplish a great deal today if you find the correct helpers.

(C) Venus leaves the Masculine Ruling (Dynamic Social) Sign of Libra for its Feminine Detriment (Responsive Personal) Sign of Scorpio. Be more strategic and self-protective in your relationships.

(D) Neptune turns Direct in Pisces. Having this prosperity Planet moving forward again is another check in the box for a prosperous economy. Good for hydro-electric and water-based wind energy.

(E) This White Circle Day combines a supportive Sagittarius Sun Sextile the Libra Moon, an uplifting connection, with a very practical Trine between Mercury and Jupiter. Don't plan to rush any discussions today. Between the slowing Mercury and the Libra Moon, fairness and consideration of everyone's point of view is essential. Good for the Air Signs.

(F) The New Moon in Sagittarius is complicated by Mercury in Capricorn turning Retrograde until January 3, 2024, so expect turbulence and communication glitches. Sagittarius, chill out!

(G) The Sun enters Capricorn as Mercury Sextiles Saturn so there is a strong practical theme as the calendar year is wrapping up. This is a good time to review your long-term ambitions. (And order your new Planetary Calendar for 2024) Good for the Earth Signs.

(H) Mercury backs into Sagittarius at the same time as it Conjuncts the Sun, so there may be travel delays and communication issues. This is hardest on the Fire Signs, Aries, Leo and Sagittarius.

(I) The Full Moon between Capricorn and Cancer is complicated by Mercury being Square Neptune so use your logic and intuition together to plan the future year.

(J) This is a lovely but busy day. It has an optimistic but practical Capricorn Sun, Trine Jupiter in Taurus, while Mercury Conjuncts Mars and Uranus makes a supportive Aspect to the Moon. This is an especially good time for Capricorn, Cancer and Sagittarius to start projects.

(K) Venus enters Sagittarius so be hopeful about love and friendship for the future. Expand your social circle outside of your closely held comfort zone. Sagittarius will feel especially charming!

(L) The Leo Moon, being supported by Mercury and Mars in Sagittarius, adds an upbeat note while Jupiter turns Direct promising to open the doors of prosperity in the coming year. *Happy New Year!*

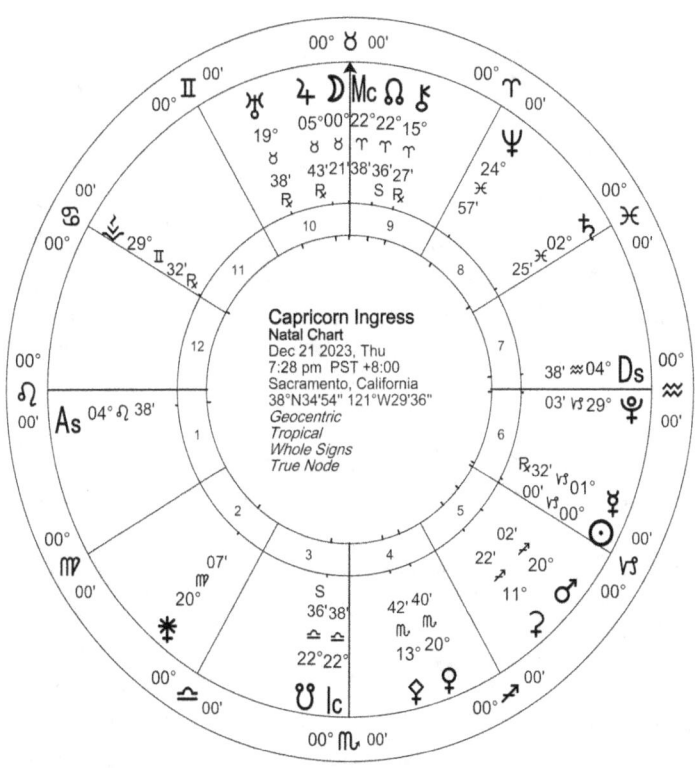

Signs

♈ Aries Begins
♉ Taurus Owns
♊ Gemini Engages
♋ Cancer Nurtures
♌ Leo Embraces
♍ Virgo Improves
♎ Libra Commits
♏ Scorpio Manages
♐ Sagittarius Views
♑ Capricorn Climbs
♒ Aquarius Herds
♓ Pisces Dreams

Planets

☉ Sun Spirit
☽ Moon Emotes
☿ Mercury Thinks
♀ Venus Feels
♂ Mars Acts
♃ Jupiter Expands
♄ Saturn Contracts
♅ Uranus Disrupts
♆ Neptune Envisions
♇ Pluto Unearths

Aspects

☌ Conjunct 0° Aligns
∥ Parallel 0° Equals
✶ Sextile 60° Helps
□ Square 90° Works
△ Trine 120° Supports
☍ Opposition 180° Counters

Sage Sagittarius says "I Foresee"

Astro Notes:

DECEMBER 2023

Sunday	Monday	Tuesday
New Year's Eve ♃ ♄ ☽♍ **31** 3:53am ♀♄ -------- 3:53am		
☽♍ **3** 7:50pm ♅♄ 6:11pm - 7:50pm ♀□♇	3rd Quarter ☽ 9:49pm ♀ Enters ♏ 10:50am C ☿♃♃ ☽♍ **4** ☉□☽ ♂	☽♍ **5** ♀△♄ ♆
♆♂ ☽♏ **10** ♅	♇♇☿ ☿✶♀ ☽♐ **11** ☉∥♇ 3:10am ♄ 12:57am - 3:10am	New ☽ 3:32pm 20° ♐ ☉♂ F ♂ ☉∥♇ ☽♐ **12** ♀∥♄ ♆ ☿Rx 10:48pm --------
♀♄♃☿♄ ☽♓ **17** ☉✶☽ 11:58am 4:03am - 11:58am	♀♅ ☽♓ **18** ☿△♃ ♂	1st Quarter ☽ 10:39am ♆♆♇ ☽♈ **19** ☉□☽ 2:46pm ☿ 1:03pm - 2:46pm
Christmas Eve ☽♊ **24** ☉✶♄ 12:14am ♄ -------- 12:14am	Christmas Day ☽♊ **25** ♀△♆ ♂♆☿ 11:55pm --------	Full ☽ 4:33pm 4° ♋ Kwanzaa (1st Day) I ♄♃ ☽♋ **26** ☉☍☽ 7:14am ☿□♆ -------- 7:14am

All calculations are Pacific Clock Time (PST & PDT)

December 2023

Mercury☿ 29° Sagittarius♐ enters Capricorn♑ on the 1st at 6:31am, turns Rx on the 12th at 11:08pm at 8° Capricorn♑, enters Sagittarius♐ on the 22nd at 10:17pm. Venus♀ 25° Libra♎ enters Scorpio♏ on the 4th at 10:50am, enters Sagittarius♐ on the 29th at 12:23pm. Mars♂ 4° Sagittarius♐. Jupiter♃ Rx 7° Taurus♉ turns Direct on the 30th at 6:40pm at 5° Taurus♉. Saturn♄ 1° Pisces♓. Uranus♅Rx 20° Taurus♉. Neptune♆Rx 24° Pisces♓ turns Direct on the 6th at 5:21am at 24° Pisces♓. Pluto♇ 28° Capricorn♑.

Wednesday	Thursday	Friday	Saturday
		☿ Enters ♑ 6:31am A ♂ ☽♌ 1 8:00am ♀♇♃ 5:06am - 8:00am	B ☿✶♄ ☉△☽ ☽♌ 2
St. Nicholas Day D ♇ ♆ 'D' ☽♎ 6 8:34am ☿ 5:50am - 8:34am	E ♂♆ ☿△♃ ☉✶☽ ☽♎ 7	Chanukah (1st Day) ♀♄♄ ☽♏ 8 7:34pm ♇ 5:05pm - 7:34pm	♀☿ ☽♏ 9 ♀☍♃ ♃
Geminid Meteors ♄♃☿ ☽♑ 13 7:31am ---------- 7:31am	Geminid Meteors ♀♅ ☽♑ 14	Chanukah (Last Day) ♆♇☿♇♂ ☉∥☽ ☉∥☿ ☽♒ 15 9:55am ♃ 8:03am - 9:55am	♂ ☿∥♇ ☿∥♂ ♂∥♇ ☉□♆ ☽♒ 16 ♀♅
☽♈ 20 ☉∥♂ ♀☍♅	☉ Enters ♑ 7:28pm Ursid Meteors G ♂♃☿♄ ☉△☽ ☿✶♄ ☽♉ 21 6:49pm ♇ Winter Solstice 6:46pm - 6:49pm	☿Rx Enters ♐ 10:17pm Ursid Meteors H ♃♅ ☽♉ 22 ☉☌☿	♅♆♇ ☽♉ 23 ♀ 10:39pm -------
J ♅ ☿☌♂ ☉△♃ ☽♋ 27	♆♀ ☽♌ 28 ♀✶♇ ♂□♆ 4:22pm ♇ 2:57pm - 4:22pm	♀ Enters ♐ 12:23pm K ☽♌ 29 ♃	L ☿♂ ☽♌ 30 ♃ 'D' ♅ 9:18pm -------

Add 1 Hour for Mountain Time (MT) - Add 2 Hours for Central Time (CT) - Add 3 Hours for Eastern Time (ET)

November into December 2023

Monday

Full ☽ 1:16am 4° ♊

K
☽ ♊ **27**
☉ ☌ ☽
☿ □ ♆

Cyber Monday

Tuesday

♀
☽ ♋ **28**
10:53pm ♆ ☿

5:02pm - 10:53pm

Wednesday

♄ ♃
☽ ♋ **29**

Thursday

♅ ♆
☽ ♋ **30**

November 27 thru December 3

Friday
☿ Enters ♑ 6:31am

A
☽♌ **1** ♂
8:00am ♀ ⚷ ♃
5:06am - 8:00am

Saturday

B
☽♌ **2** ☿✶♄
☉△☽

Sunday
☽♍ **3** ♀
7:50pm ♅♄ ♀□⚷
6:11pm - 7:50pm

189

December 2023

Monday
3rd Quarter ☽ 9:49pm
♀ Enters ♏ 10:50am

C ☿ ♃

☽♍ **4**
⊙□☽
♂

Tuesday

☽♍ **5** ♀△♄
♅
♆

Wednesday
St. Nicholas Day

D ℙ
☽♎ **6** ♆ 'D'
8:34am ☿

5:50am - 8:34am

Thursday

E ♂♆ ☿△♃
☽♎ **7** ⊙✳☽

December 4 thru 10

Friday

Chanukah (1st Day)

☽♏ **8** ♀♄♄
7:34pm ♇

5:05pm - 7:34pm

Saturday

☽♏ **9** ♀☿
♃ ♀☍♃

Sunday

☽♏ **10** ♆♂
♅

December 2023

Monday

☽ ♐
3:10am

♇♇☿ ☿✳♀
11 ⊙∥☽
♄

12:57am – 3:10am

Tuesday

New ☽ 3:32pm 20° ♐

F

☽ ♐
12
♆

♂ ⊙☌☽
⊙∥♇
♀∥♄
☿Rx

10:48pm

Wednesday

Geminid Meteors

☽ ♑
13
7:31am

♄ ♃ ☿

————— 7:31am

Thursday

Geminid Meteors

☽ ♑
14

♀ ♅

December 11 thru 17

Friday

Chanukah (Last Day)

☽≈ **15** ΨPȢPσ ☉∥☽
9:55am ☉∥☿
♃
8:03am - 9:55am

Saturday

☽≈ **16** σ ☿∥P
♀♅ ☿∥σ
σ∥P
☉□Ψ

Sunday

☽H **17** ♀♄♃☿♄
11:58am ☉✶☽

4:03am - 11:58am

December 2023

Monday
☽ ♓ **18** ♀☿
☿△♃
♂

Tuesday
1st Quarter ☽ 10:39am

☽ ♈ **19** Ψ Ψ P
⊙□☽
2:46pm ☿

1:03pm - 2:46pm

Wednesday
☽ ♈ **20** ⊙∥♂
♀☌♅

Thursday
⊙ Enters ♑ 7:28pm
Ursid Meteors
G ♂♃ ☿♄ ⊙△☽
☽ ♉ **21** ☿⚹♄
6:49pm P
Winter Solstice
6:46pm - 6:49pm

December 18 thru 24

Friday

☿Rx Enters ♐ 10:17pm
Ursid Meteors

☽♉ **H 22** ♃♅ ☉☌☿

Saturday

☽♉ **23** ♅♆♇ ♀

10:39pm

Sunday
Christmas Eve

☽♊ **24** ☉⚹♄
12:14am ♄

--------- 12:14am

December 2023

Monday
Christmas Day

☽ ♊ **25** ♀△♆
♂♆☿
11:55pm

Tuesday
Full ☽ 4:33pm 4° ♋
Kwanzaa (1st Day)
I ♄ ♃
☽ ♋ **26** ☉☍☽
7:14am ☿□♆
-------- 7:14am

Wednesday
J ♅ ☿☌♂
☽ ♋ **27** ☉△♃

Thursday
♆♀
☽ ♌ **28** ♀✶♇
♂□♆
4:22pm ♇
2:57pm - 4:22pm

December 25 thru 31

Friday
♀ Enters ♐ 12:23pm

K
☽ ☊ **29**
♃

Saturday

L
☽ ☊ **30** ☿ ♂   ♃ 'D'
♅
9:18pm

Sunday
New Year's Eve

♃ ♃
☽ ♍ **31**
3:53am ♀ ♄
---------- 3:53am

Here's a Peek at 2024!

In this Year of the Wood Dragon, the global focus will be the legal and political chaos around the USA elections. While Jupiter Sextile Saturn promotes a solid economy, American commodities, agriculture, and financial markets will be leading the way. Currency innovation will grow but bring with it cyber manipulation. Cuba and Florida are facing challenges politically and environmentally requiring government expenditures, and innovation in civic and building technology, adapting to rising ocean levels. Europe will withdraw into their own affairs while the Pacific Rim economies will see growth and increased exchange among that community. Our video Forecasts are at www.PlanetaryCalendar.com/forecasts

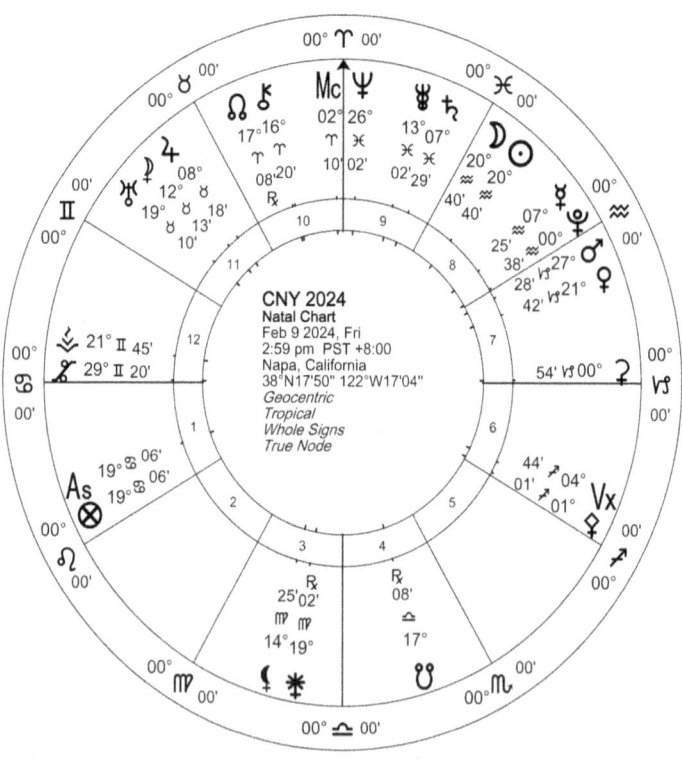

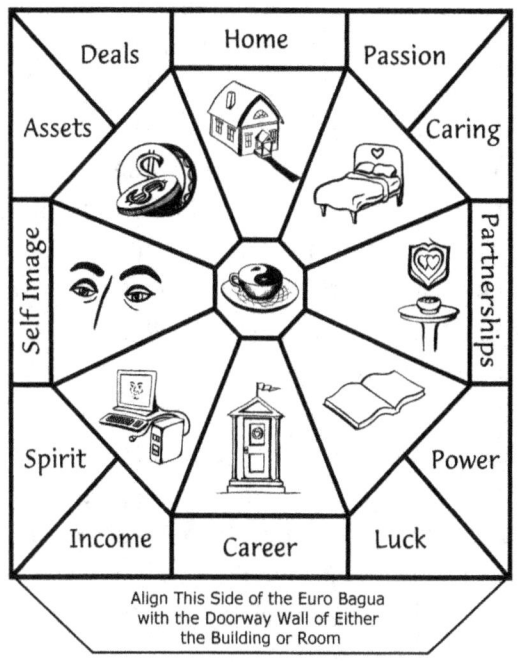

Align This Side of the Euro Bagua with the Doorway Wall of Either the Building or Room

NINE: HEALING WITH THE TERRA MAP

We would like to introduce you to a unique part of the starry arts called Location Astrology, where we use the 'Terra Map' to correlate the 12 Signs and Houses with a room or a building's layout. This map reveals the pattern of the planetary energy you imprint on your space, as a tool for you to heal that space and your life. You use the map by aligning it with the wall that contains the entrance to the room.

Look at the areas of your life and determine what could use a little boost or a some calming down. Then apply adjustments in the form of color, sound, movement and scent to enhance that part of your life. In the video we expand on the keywords related to each Zodiac Sign connected to each section, and you should add your own ideas and keywords from your unique life experience.

When standing in the entrance, looking into the room, the far-left corner shows the condition of your finances and the far-right corner shows the condition of your love life. Get them right and everything else falls into place! The front wall **(#9, 10 & 11)** relates to your social world, while the back wall **(#3, 4 & 5)** relates to your personal life. The middle of the left wall **(#1)** relates to your self-image while the opposite spot (#7) relates to your partnerships. **(#2)** & **(#6)** are your talents and where they are put to use. **(#8)** & **(#9)** are where the unseen sneaks up on you.

You don't have to be a Leo to have a romance section **(#5)** and if that's where your clothes hamper is kept, it should be no wonder that the joy factor in your life could use a little boost. Putting roses there, a painting of roses or rose oil, you get the picture, should add some much needed 'heart energy' to this area.

We like to suggest essential oils and crystals because they are easy to use, even if the architect who created your space may not have considered your love life important enough to allow for a table, or wall space for other cures. We have included oils on the included map for each section with the video.

In choosing cures what you like most rules, and you can always get good results using clear, terminated crystals with citrus oils like lemon, orange, grapefruit or bergamot to boost energy and florals like jasmine, rose and gardenia for balancing the energy.

When choosing essential oils to go with the Signs and Houses, the main guidance comes from their Ruling Planet. Why? Because while the Signs represent time, in the form of the twelve segments that make up the four seasons, the Planets represent the physical embodiment of those energies. Also, oils are complex, and while they will have a core theme, they include diverse components.

So, an oil or crystal that relates to Venus, may be used for either Taurus or Libra. So, the Venusian oil Neroli works well in both the Second and Seventh Terra Houses. Those related to Mars may be used for Aries or Scorpio, so Cinnamon oil work well in both the First and Eighth Houses, and so on. Even the Sun and the Moon can exchange oils and crystals, for example Rose oil works well in both the Fourth and Fifth Houses.

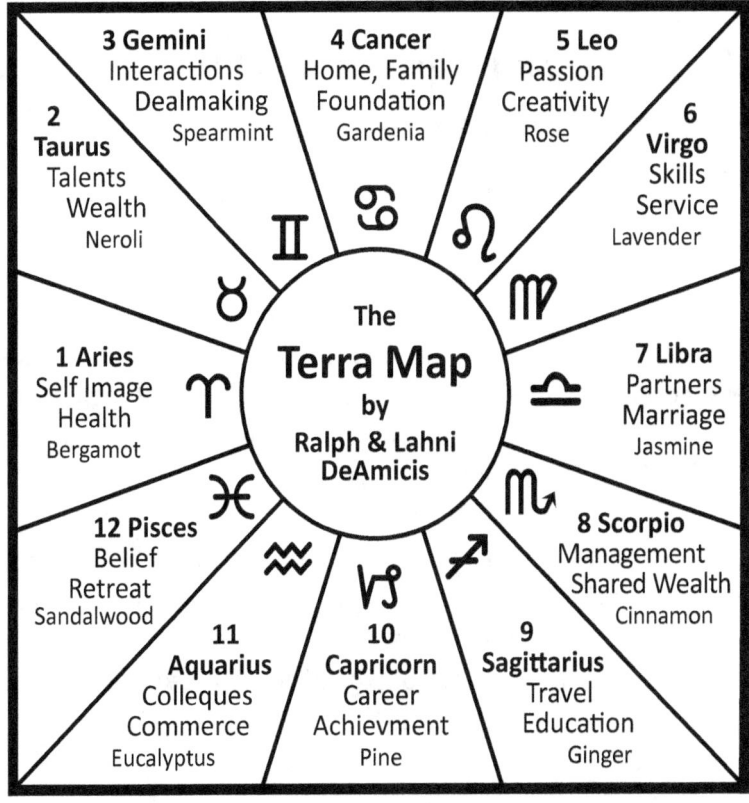

The Entrance is in Section 9, 10 or 11. Align this Bottom Edge with the Primary Entrance Wall to the Room or Building.

Feng Shui Tips for Good Health
From Ralph & Lahni's Book
Feng Shui & the Tango in 12 Easy Lessons

1: When you hang a chime or a bell on your main entrance/exit doors, you gain control of the environment. Doors are the mouth to any outside energy and the person who controls access, commands the space. When the bell rings it signals an alert, providing increased protection from outside invaders, whether human, animal or energetic.

2: It is imperative that you do not sleep with your head pointing towards the South. North is best. Why? The Electro Magnetic Field of the Earth flows from North to South and your personal field flows from your head to your feet. With your head pointing North, the Earth's current strokes your field with the grain.

With your head in the south, it brushes against the grain and, with time, it can reverse your field's direction, making everything in life that much harder. Pointing your head West or East works in a pinch. If you can only place your headboard to the South, sleep with your head at the footboard. Your health will thank us for that.

3: Never bring your shoes into your bedroom. The soles come into contact with too much negativity out there and then you place them under your bed, wondering why you relive the worst parts of your day, your dreams are wonky, or you can't sleep at all. Lock them in the closet or better yet, leave them by the front door.

4: Standing water attracts energy. Don't let the standing water in your bathroom drain your strength and resources. Shut the lid, and the door, so the Feng Shui Police don't have to write you a ticket. If you have a connected bathroom, you will find that you no longer wake up feeling more 'drained' than when you went to sleep.

5: Electro Magnetics in many bedrooms are out of control. You can practically read by the lights from all those little LEDs. Your bedroom should be an 'unplugged zone' so you can 'recharge' with the Earth's natural current. The first thing to go is that electric alarm clock next to your head. It is an easy switch to a battery-operated travel alarm, that uses a Direct Current, like the human body, and unlike the common Alternating Current which leaves you frazzled.

*Moon Signs are Calculated for
Noon Pacific Time
Order Your 2024 Planner at
www.PlanetaryCalendar.com*

JANUARY 2024

Moon Positions are for Noon Pacific Time

Sunday	Monday	Tuesday	Wednesday	Thursday	Friday	Saturday
New Year's Day	☽♍ 1	☽♍ 2	☽♎ 3	☽♎ 4	Epiphany ☽♏ 5	☽♏ 6
☽♏ 7	☽♐ 8	☽♐ 9	☽♐ 10	☽♑ 11	☽♒ 12	☽♒ 13
☽♓ 14	Martin Luther King Day ☽♓ 15	☽♈ 16	☽♈ 17	☽♉ 18	☽♉ 19	☽♊ 20
Chinese New Year ☽♊ 21	☽♊ 22	☽♋ 23	☽♋ 24	☽♌ 25	☽♌ 26	☽♍ 27
☽♍ 28	☽♍ 29	☽♎ 30	☽♎ 31			

January 2023 Ephemeris

00:00 UT

Day	Sid.t	☉	☽	☿	♀	♂	♃	♄	♅	♆	♇	☊	⚷	⚸	Day
S 1	6 41 33	10♑17'02	3♐39	23°R42	27♑23	9♈R 4	1♈12	22≈25	15°R 9	22♓52	27♑39	11♉45	10♉12	29♋ 9	11♈58	S 1
M 2	6 45 30	11°18'11	16♏14	23♐ 6	28°38	8Ⅱ55	1°19	22°31	15♉ 8	22°53	27°41	11°R45	10° 9	29°16	11°59	M 2
T 3	6 49 26	12°19'19	28°36	22°18	29°53	8°46	1°26	22°37	15° 7	22°54	27°43	11°44	10° 6	29°23	11°59	T 3
W 4	6 53 23	13°20'27	10Ⅱ48	21°20	1≈ 8	8°39	1°34	22°43	15° 6	22°55	27°45	11°40	10° 3	29°29	12° 0	W 4
T 5	6 57 20	14°21'35	22°53	20°13	2°23	8°32	1°42	22°49	15° 5	22°56	27°47	11°33	10° 0	29°36	12° 1	T 5
F 6	7 1 16	15°22'43	4♋52	18°59	3°39	8°26	1°50	22°56	15° 4	22°57	27°49	11°23	9°56	29°43	12° 1	F 6
S 7	7 5 13	16°23'51	16°47	17°40	4°54	8°21	1°58	23° 2	15° 3	22°59	27°51	11°11	9°53	29°49	12° 2	S 7
S 8	7 9 9	17°24'59	28°41	16°20	6° 9	8°17	2° 6	23° 8	15° 2	23° 0	27°53	10°58	9°50	29°56	12° 3	S 8
M 9	7 13 6	18°26'06	10♌33	15° 0	7°24	8°14	2°14	23°15	15° 1	23° 1	27°55	10°45	9°47	0♌ 3	12° 4	M 9
T10	7 17 2	19°27'14	22°26	13°42	8°39	8°11	2°23	23°21	15° 1	23° 2	27°57	10°32	9°44	0°10	12° 5	T10
W11	7 20 59	20°28'21	4♍21	12°31	9°54	8° 9	2°32	23°28	15° 0	23° 3	27°59	10°21	9°40	0°16	12° 6	W11
T12	7 24 55	21°29'29	16°21	11°26	11° 9	8° 8	2°40	23°34	15° 0	23° 5	28° 1	10°13	9°37	0°23	12° 7	T12
F13	7 28 52	22°30'36	28°30	10°30	12°24	8°D 8	2°49	23°41	14°59	23° 6	28° 3	10° 8	9°34	0°30	12° 8	F13
S14	7 32 49	23°31'43	10♎51	9°42	13°39	8° 8	2°58	23°47	14°59	23° 7	28° 5	10° 5	9°31	0°36	12° 9	S14
S15	7 36 45	24°32'50	23°29	9° 5	14°54	8° 9	3° 8	23°54	14°58	23° 9	28° 7	10°D 5	9°28	0°43	12°10	S15
M16	7 40 42	25°33'57	6♏28	8°37	16° 9	8°11	3°17	24° 7	14°58	23°10	28° 9	10°R 5	9°25	0°50	12°11	M16
T17	7 44 38	26°35'04	19°53	8°19	17°24	8°14	3°26	24° 7	14°57	23°11	28°11	10° 4	9°21	0°57	12°13	T17
W18	7 48 35	27°36'10	3♐47	8° 9	18°39	8°18	3°36	24°14	14°57	23°13	28°12	10° 3	9°18	1° 3	12°14	W18
T19	7 52 31	28°37'17	18°10	8°D 9	19°54	8°22	3°46	24°21	14°57	23°14	28°14	9°58	9°15	1°10	12°15	T19
F20	7 56 28	29°38'23	2♑57	8°17	21° 8	8°27	3°56	24°27	14°57	23°16	28°16	9°51	9°12	1°17	12°17	F20
S21	8 0 24	0≈39'29	18°11	8°32	22°23	8°32	4° 6	24°34	14°57	23°17	28°18	9°41	9° 9	1°24	12°18	S21
S22	8 4 21	1°40'34	3≈32	8°54	23°38	8°39	4°16	24°41	14°56	23°19	28°20	9°30	9° 6	1°30	12°20	S22
M23	8 8 18	2°41'38	18°53	9°22	24°53	8°46	4°26	24°48	14°D56	23°21	28°22	9°18	9° 2	1°37	12°22	M23
T24	8 12 14	3°42'42	4♓ 1	9°56	26° 8	8°53	4°36	24°55	14°56	23°22	28°24	9° 8	8°59	1°44	12°23	T24
W25	8 16 11	4°43'44	18°46	10°35	27°23	9° 2	4°47	25° 2	14°57	23°24	28°26	8°59	8°56	1°50	12°25	W25
T26	8 20 7	5°44'46	3♈ 3	11°19	28°37	9°10	4°57	25° 9	14°57	23°25	28°28	8°54	8°53	1°57	12°27	T26
F27	8 24 4	6°45'46	16°51	12° 7	29°52	9°20	5° 8	25°16	14°57	23°27	28°30	8°51	8°50	2° 4	12°28	F27
S28	8 28 0	7°46'45	0♉10	12°58	1♓ 7	9°30	5°19	25°23	14°57	23°29	28°32	8°50	8°46	2°11	12°30	S28
S29	8 31 57	8°47'44	13° 3	13°54	2°21	9°41	5°30	25°30	14°57	23°31	28°34	8°50	8°43	2°17	12°32	S29
M30	8 35 53	9°48'41	25°35	14°52	3°36	9°52	5°41	25°37	14°58	23°32	28°36	8°49	8°40	2°24	12°34	M30
T31	8 39 50	10≈49'37	7Ⅱ51	15≈53	4♓51	10Ⅱ 4	5♈52	25≈44	14♉58	23♓34	28♑38	8♉47	8♉37	2♌31	12♈36	T31

205

February 2023
Ephemeris

FEBRUARY 2023 **00:00 UT**

Day	Sid.t	☉	☽	☿	♀	♂	♃	♄	♅	♆	♇	☊	☊	⚸	⚷	Day
W 1	8 43 47	11♒50'31	19♊56	16♑57	6♓ 5	10♊17	6♈ 3	25♒51	14♉59	23♓36	28♑40	8°R42	8♉34	2♌38	12♈38	W 1
T 2	8 47 43	12°51'25	1♋54	18° 3	7°20	10°30	6°15	25°58	14°59	23°38	28°42	8♉35	8°31	2°44	12°40	T 2
F 3	8 51 40	13°52'17	13°47	19°12	8°34	10°43	6°26	26° 5	15° 0	23°40	28°44	8°24	8°27	2°51	12°42	F 3
S 4	8 55 36	14°53'08	25°39	20°22	9°49	10°57	6°38	26°13	15° 0	23°41	28°46	8°11	8°24	2°58	12°45	S 4
S 5	8 59 33	15°53'58	7♌31	21°35	11° 3	11°12	6°49	26°20	15° 1	23°43	28°48	7°56	8°21	3° 4	12°47	S 5
M 6	9 3 29	16°54'46	19°25	22°49	12°18	11°27	7° 1	26°27	15° 2	23°45	28°49	7°41	8°18	3°11	12°49	M 6
T 7	9 7 26	17°55'34	1♍23	24° 4	13°32	11°43	7°13	26°34	15° 2	23°47	28°51	7°27	8°15	3°18	12°51	T 7
W 8	9 11 22	18°56'20	13°25	25°21	14°46	11°59	7°25	26°41	15° 3	23°49	28°53	7°15	8°12	3°25	12°54	W 8
T 9	9 15 19	19°57'05	25°32	26°40	16° 1	12°15	7°37	26°48	15° 4	23°51	28°55	7° 6	8° 8	3°31	12°56	T 9
F 10	9 19 16	20°57'49	7♎48	28° 0	17°15	12°32	7°49	26°56	15° 5	23°53	28°57	7° 0	8° 5	3°38	12°58	F 10
S 11	9 23 12	21°58'32	20°13	29°21	18°29	12°49	8° 1	27° 3	15° 6	23°55	28°59	6°56	8° 2	3°45	13° 1	S 11
S 12	9 27 9	22°59'14	2♏53	0♒43	19°43	13° 7	8°13	27°10	15° 7	23°57	29° 1	6°D55	7°59	3°51	13° 3	S 12
M13	9 31 5	23°59'54	15°50	2° 7	20°58	13°25	8°25	27°17	15° 8	23°59	29° 2	6°55	7°56	3°58	13° 6	M13
T 14	9 35 2	25° 0'34	29° 9	3°32	22°12	13°44	8°38	27°25	15° 9	24° 1	29° 4	6°R55	7°52	4° 5	13° 8	T 14
W15	9 38 58	26° 1'13	12♐51	4°57	23°26	14° 3	8°50	27°32	15°10	24° 3	29° 6	6°54	7°49	4°12	13°11	W15
T 16	9 42 55	27° 1'51	27° 0	6°24	24°40	14°22	9° 3	27°39	15°12	24° 5	29° 8	6°51	7°46	4°18	13°14	T 16
F 17	9 46 51	28° 2'27	11♑34	7°52	25°54	14°42	9°15	27°46	15°13	24° 7	29°10	6°45	7°43	4°25	13°16	F 17
S 18	9 50 48	29° 3'02	26°30	9°21	27° 8	15° 2	9°28	27°54	15°14	24° 9	29°11	6°37	7°40	4°32	13°19	S 18
S 19	9 54 45	0♓ 3'36	11♒39	10°51	28°22	15°23	9°41	28° 1	15°16	24°11	29°13	6°27	7°37	4°39	13°22	S 19
M20	9 58 41	1° 4'09	26°53	12°22	29°36	15°44	9°54	28° 8	15°17	24°14	29°15	6°17	7°33	4°45	13°24	M20
T 21	10 2 38	2° 4'39	11♓59	13°53	0♈49	16° 5	10° 7	28°15	15°18	24°16	29°17	6° 7	7°30	4°52	13°27	T 21
W22	10 6 34	3° 5'09	26°49	15°26	2° 3	16°27	10°20	28°23	15°20	24°18	29°18	5°59	7°27	4°59	13°30	W22
T 23	10 10 31	4° 5'36	11♈14	17° 0	3°17	16°49	10°33	28°30	15°21	24°20	29°20	5°54	7°24	5° 5	13°33	T 23
F 24	10 14 27	5° 6'01	25°11	18°35	4°31	17°11	10°46	28°37	15°23	24°22	29°22	5°52	7°21	5°12	13°36	F 24
S 25	10 18 24	6° 6'25	8♉39	20°10	5°44	17°33	10°59	28°44	15°25	24°24	29°23	5°D51	7°17	5°19	13°39	S 25
S 26	10 22 20	7° 6'47	21°39	21°47	6°58	17°56	11°12	28°52	15°26	24°27	29°25	5°52	7°14	5°26	13°42	S 26
M27	10 26 17	8° 7'07	4♊17	23°24	8°11	18°19	11°25	28°59	15°28	24°29	29°26	5°R53	7°11	5°32	13°45	M27
T 28	10 30 14	9♓ 7'25	16♊35	25♒ 3	9♈25	18♊43	11♈39	29♒ 6	15♉30	24♓31	29♑28	5♉53	7♉ 8	5♌39	13♈48	T 28

March 2023 Ephemeris

MARCH 2023 **00:00 UT**

Day	Sid.t	☉	☽	☿	♀	♂	♃	♄	♅	♆	♇	☊	☊	⚸	⚷	Day
W 1	10 34 10	10♓ 7'41	28♊40	26♒43	10♈38	19♊ 7	11♈52	29♒13	15♉32	24♓33	29♑30	5°R50	7♉ 5	5♌46	13♈51	W 1
T 2	10 38 7	11° 7'55	10♋36	28°23	11°52	19°31	12° 6	29°20	15°34	24°35	29°31	5♉46	7° 2	5°53	13°54	T 2
F 3	10 42 3	12° 8'06	22°28	0♓ 5	13° 5	19°55	12°19	29°28	15°36	24°38	29°33	5°40	6°58	5°59	13°57	F 3
S 4	10 46 0	13° 8'16	4♌19	1°48	14°18	20°19	12°33	29°35	15°38	24°40	29°34	5°31	6°55	6° 6	14° 0	S 4
S 5	10 49 56	14° 8'24	16°12	3°31	15°31	20°44	12°46	29°42	15°40	24°42	29°36	5°21	6°52	6°13	14° 3	S 5
M 6	10 53 53	15° 8'30	28°11	5°16	16°44	21° 9	13° 0	29°49	15°42	24°44	29°37	5°11	6°49	6°19	14° 6	M 6
T 7	10 57 49	16° 8'34	10♍15	7° 2	17°58	21°35	13°14	29°56	15°44	24°47	29°39	5° 1	6°46	6°26	14°10	T 7
W 8	11 1 46	17° 8'36	22°27	8°49	19°10	22° 0	13°27	0♓ 3	15°46	24°49	29°40	4°53	6°43	6°33	14°13	W 8
T 9	11 5 43	18° 8'36	4♎47	10°37	20°23	22°26	13°41	0°10	15°48	24°51	29°42	4°47	6°39	6°40	14°16	T 9
F 10	11 9 39	19° 8'35	17°17	12°26	21°36	22°52	13°55	0°17	15°50	24°53	29°43	4°43	6°36	6°46	14°19	F 10
S 11	11 13 36	20° 8'32	29°57	14°17	22°49	23°18	14° 9	0°24	15°52	24°56	29°44	4°D42	6°33	6°53	14°23	S 11
S 12	11 17 32	21° 8'26	12♏50	16° 8	24° 2	23°45	14°23	0°31	15°55	24°58	29°46	4°42	6°30	7° 0	14°26	S 12
M13	11 21 29	22° 8'20	25°56	18° 1	25°14	24°11	14°37	0°38	15°57	25° 0	29°47	4°43	6°27	7° 6	14°29	M13
T 14	11 25 25	23° 8'12	9♐19	19°54	26°27	24°38	14°51	0°45	15°59	25° 2	29°49	4°45	6°23	7°13	14°32	T 14
W15	11 29 22	24° 8'02	22°59	21°49	27°39	25° 5	15° 5	0°52	16° 2	25° 5	29°50	4°R45	6°20	7°20	14°36	W15
T 16	11 33 18	25° 7'50	6♑59	23°45	28°52	25°32	15°19	0°59	16° 4	25° 7	29°51	4°45	6°17	7°27	14°39	T 16
F 17	11 37 15	26° 7'37	21°17	25°42	0♉ 4	26° 0	15°33	1° 6	16° 7	25° 9	29°52	4°42	6°14	7°33	14°43	F 17
S 18	11 41 12	27° 7'22	5♒51	27°40	1°17	26°27	15°47	1°12	16° 9	25°12	29°54	4°38	6°11	7°40	14°46	S 18
S 19	11 45 8	28° 7'06	20°36	29°38	2°29	26°55	16° 1	1°19	16°12	25°14	29°55	4°33	6° 8	7°47	14°49	S 19
M20	11 49 5	29° 6'47	5♓27	1♈38	3°41	27°23	16°15	1°26	16°14	25°16	29°56	4°28	6° 4	7°54	14°53	M20
T 21	11 53 1	0♈ 6'27	20°14	3°38	4°53	27°51	16°30	1°33	16°17	25°18	29°57	4°23	6° 1	8° 0	14°56	T 21
W22	11 56 58	1° 6'04	4♈49	5°38	6° 5	28°20	16°44	1°39	16°20	25°21	29°58	4°19	5°58	8° 7	15° 0	W22
T 23	12 0 54	2° 5'40	19° 7	7°39	7°17	28°48	16°58	1°46	16°22	25°23	29°59	4°16	5°55	8°14	15° 3	T 23
F 24	12 4 51	3° 5'13	3♉ 2	9°40	8°29	29°17	17°12	1°52	16°25	25°25	0♒ 1	4°D15	5°52	8°20	15° 7	F 24
S 25	12 8 47	4° 4'45	16°32	11°41	9°41	29°46	17°27	1°59	16°28	25°27	0° 2	4°16	5°49	8°27	15°10	S 25
S 26	12 12 44	5° 4'14	29°38	13°41	10°52	0♋15	17°41	2° 5	16°31	25°30	0° 3	4°17	5°45	8°34	15°13	S 26
M27	12 16 41	6° 3'41	12♊20	15°41	12° 4	0°44	17°55	2°12	16°33	25°32	0° 4	4°19	5°42	8°41	15°17	M27
T 28	12 20 37	7° 3'06	24°44	17°40	13°15	1°13	18°10	2°18	16°36	25°34	0° 5	4°20	5°39	8°47	15°20	T 28
W29	12 24 34	8° 2'28	6♋52	19°38	14°27	1°43	18°24	2°25	16°39	25°36	0° 6	4°R21	5°36	8°54	15°24	W29
T 30	12 28 30	9° 1'48	18°51	21°33	15°38	2°12	18°38	2°31	16°42	25°39	0° 7	4°20	5°33	9° 1	15°27	T 30
F 31	12 32 27	10♈ 1'06	0♌44	23♈27	16♉49	2♋42	18♈53	2♓37	16♉45	25♓41	0♒ 7	4♉19	5♉29	9♌ 7	15♈31	F 31

April 2023
Ephemeris

APRIL 2023 **00:00 UT**

Day	Sid.t	☉	☽	☿	♀	♂	♃	♄	♅	♆	♇	☊	☊	⚸	⚷	Day
S 1	12 36 23	11♈ 0'21	12♌36	25♈18	18♉ 1	3♋12	19♈ 7	2♓44	16♉48	25♓43	0♒ 8	4°R16	5♉26	9♌14	15♈35	S 1
S 2	12 40 20	11°59'34	24°31	27° 6	19°12	3°42	19°22	2°50	16°51	25°45	0° 9	4♉13	5°23	9°21	15°38	S 2
M 3	12 44 16	12°58'45	6♍33	28°51	20°22	4°12	19°36	2°56	16°54	25°48	0°10	4° 9	5°20	9°28	15°42	M 3
T 4	12 48 13	13°57'54	18°45	0♉32	21°33	4°42	19°51	3° 2	16°57	25°50	0°11	4° 6	5°17	9°34	15°45	T 4
W 5	12 52 9	14°57'00	1♎ 7	2° 9	22°44	5°13	20° 5	3° 8	17° 0	25°52	0°12	4° 3	5°14	9°41	15°49	W 5
T 6	12 56 6	15°56'05	13°42	3°41	23°55	5°43	20°19	3°14	17° 3	25°54	0°12	4° 1	5°10	9°48	15°52	T 6
F 7	13 0 3	16°55'07	26°30	5° 9	25° 5	6°14	20°34	3°20	17° 6	25°56	0°13	4° 0	5° 7	9°55	15°56	F 7
S 8	13 3 59	17°54'07	9♏32	6°32	26°16	6°45	20°48	3°26	17° 9	25°58	0°14	4°D 0	5° 4	10° 1	15°59	S 8
S 9	13 7 56	18°53'06	22°46	7°49	27°26	7°16	21° 3	3°32	17°12	26° 1	0°14	4° 1	5° 1	10° 8	16° 3	S 9
M10	13 11 52	19°52'02	6♐14	9° 1	28°36	7°47	21°17	3°37	17°15	26° 3	0°15	4° 2	4°58	10°15	16° 6	M10
T 11	13 15 49	20°50'57	19°53	10° 8	29°46	8°18	21°32	3°43	17°19	26° 5	0°16	4° 3	4°54	10°21	16°10	T 11
W12	13 19 45	21°49'51	3♑44	11° 8	0♊56	8°49	21°46	3°49	17°22	26° 7	0°16	4° 4	4°51	10°28	16°13	W12
T 13	13 23 42	22°48'42	17°46	12° 3	2° 6	9°20	22° 1	3°54	17°25	26° 9	0°17	4°R 4	4°48	10°35	16°17	T 13
F 14	13 27 38	23°47'32	1♒57	12°51	3°16	9°52	22°15	4° 0	17°28	26°11	0°17	4° 4	4°45	10°42	16°20	F 14
S 15	13 31 35	24°46'20	16°16	13°34	4°25	10°23	22°30	4° 5	17°32	26°13	0°18	4° 4	4°42	10°48	16°24	S 15
S 16	13 35 32	25°45'07	0♓38	14°10	5°35	10°55	22°44	4°11	17°35	26°15	0°18	4° 3	4°39	10°55	16°27	S 16
M17	13 39 28	26°43'51	15° 0	14°40	6°44	11°26	22°59	4°16	17°38	26°17	0°19	4° 2	4°35	11° 2	16°31	M17
T 18	13 43 25	27°42'34	29°19	15° 3	7°53	11°58	23°13	4°22	17°41	26°19	0°19	4° 1	4°32	11° 9	16°34	T 18
W19	13 47 21	28°41'15	13♈29	15°21	9° 2	12°30	23°28	4°27	17°45	26°21	0°20	4° 1	4°29	11°15	16°38	W19
T 20	13 51 18	29°39'54	27°25	15°32	10°11	13° 2	23°42	4°32	17°48	26°23	0°20	4°D 1	4°26	11°22	16°41	T 20
F 21	13 55 14	0♉38'31	11♉ 5	15°R37	11°20	13°34	23°57	4°37	17°51	26°25	0°20	4° 1	4°23	11°29	16°45	F 21
S 22	13 59 11	1°37'07	24°26	15°36	12°29	14° 6	24°11	4°42	17°55	26°27	0°20	4° 1	4°20	11°35	16°48	S 22
S 23	14 3 7	2°35'40	7♊27	15°30	13°37	14°39	24°25	4°47	17°58	26°29	0°21	4° 1	4°16	11°42	16°52	S 23
M24	14 7 4	3°34'12	20°10	15°18	14°46	15°11	24°40	4°52	18° 2	26°31	0°21	4°R 1	4°13	11°49	16°55	M24
T 25	14 11 1	4°32'41	2♋35	15° 0	15°54	15°43	24°54	4°57	18° 5	26°33	0°21	4° 1	4°10	11°56	16°58	T 25
W26	14 14 57	5°31'08	14°46	14°39	17° 2	16°16	25° 8	5° 2	18° 8	26°35	0°21	4° 1	4° 7	12° 2	17° 2	W26
T 27	14 18 54	6°29'33	26°46	14°13	18°10	16°49	25°23	5° 6	18°12	26°37	0°22	4° 1	4° 4	12° 9	17° 5	T 27
F 28	14 22 50	7°27'56	8♌41	13°43	19°18	17°21	25°37	5°11	18°15	26°38	0°22	4°D 1	4° 0	12°16	17° 9	F 28
S 29	14 26 47	8°26'17	20°34	13°10	20°26	17°54	25°51	5°15	18°19	26°40	0°22	4° 1	3°57	12°22	17°12	S 29
S 30	14 30 43	9♉24'36	2♍30	12♉35	21♊33	18♋27	26♈ 6	5♓20	18♉22	26♓42	0♒22	4♉ 1	3♉54	12♌29	17♈15	S 30

May 2023
Ephemeris

MAY 2023 **00:00 UT**

Day	Sid.t	☉	☽	☿	♀	♂	♃	♄	♅	♆	♇	☊	☊	⚸	⚷	Day
M 1	14 34 40	10♉22'52	14♍34	11°R57	22♊40	19♋ 0	26♈20	5♓24	18♉26	26♓44	0♒22	4♉ 2	3♉51	12♌36	17♈19	M 1
T 2	14 38 36	11°21'07	26°49	11♉19	23°48	19°33	26°34	5°29	18°29	26°46	0°R22	4° 2	3°48	12°43	17°22	T 2
W 3	14 42 33	12°19'19	9♎19	10°40	24°55	20° 6	26°48	5°33	18°32	26°47	0°22	4° 3	3°45	12°49	17°25	W 3
T 4	14 46 30	13°17'30	22° 6	10° 2	26° 1	20°39	27° 2	5°37	18°36	26°49	0°22	4° 4	3°41	12°56	17°28	T 4
F 5	14 50 26	14°15'39	5♏12	9°24	27° 8	21°12	27°17	5°41	18°39	26°51	0°22	4°R 4	3°38	13° 3	17°32	F 5
S 6	14 54 23	15°13'46	18°35	8°48	28°14	21°45	27°31	5°45	18°43	26°52	0°22	4° 4	3°35	13°10	17°35	S 6
S 7	14 58 19	16°11'52	2♐16	8°14	29°20	22°19	27°45	5°49	18°46	26°54	0°21	4° 3	3°32	13°16	17°38	S 7
M 8	15 2 16	17° 9'56	16°10	7°43	0♋26	22°52	27°59	5°53	18°50	26°56	0°21	4° 1	3°29	13°23	17°41	M 8
T 9	15 6 12	18° 7'59	0♑16	7°15	1°32	23°26	28°13	5°57	18°53	26°57	0°21	4° 0	3°26	13°30	17°44	T 9
W10	15 10 9	19° 6'00	14°29	6°50	2°38	23°59	28°27	6° 0	18°57	26°59	0°21	3°58	3°22	13°36	17°48	W10
T 11	15 14 5	20° 4'00	28°45	6°30	3°43	24°33	28°41	6° 4	19° 0	27° 0	0°21	3°56	3°19	13°43	17°51	T 11
F 12	15 18 2	21° 1'58	13♒ 2	6°13	4°48	25° 6	28°55	6° 7	19° 4	27° 2	0°20	3°56	3°16	13°50	17°54	F 12
S 13	15 21 59	21°59'55	27°15	6° 1	5°53	25°40	29° 9	6°11	19° 7	27° 3	0°20	3°D55	3°13	13°57	17°57	S 13
S 14	15 25 55	22°57'51	11♓23	5°54	6°58	26°14	29°23	6°14	19°11	27° 5	0°20	3°56	3°10	14° 3	18° 0	S 14
M15	15 29 52	23°55'46	25°24	5°D51	8° 2	26°48	29°36	6°17	19°14	27° 6	0°19	3°57	3° 6	14°10	18° 3	M15
T 16	15 33 48	24°53'39	9♈16	5°53	9° 6	27°22	29°50	6°21	19°18	27° 8	0°19	3°59	3° 3	14°17	18° 6	T 16
W17	15 37 45	25°51'31	22°58	5°59	10°10	27°56	0♉ 4	6°24	19°21	27° 9	0°19	4° 0	3° 0	14°23	18° 9	W17
T 18	15 41 41	26°49'22	6♉28	6°10	11°14	28°30	0°17	6°27	19°25	27°11	0°18	4°R 0	2°57	14°30	18°12	T 18
F 19	15 45 38	27°47'12	19°45	6°25	12°17	29° 4	0°31	6°30	19°28	27°12	0°18	3°59	2°54	14°37	18°15	F 19
S 20	15 49 34	28°45'00	2♊49	6°45	13°21	29°38	0°45	6°32	19°31	27°13	0°17	3°57	2°51	14°44	18°17	S 20
S 21	15 53 31	29°42'47	15°38	7° 9	14°24	0♌12	0°58	6°35	19°35	27°14	0°17	3°54	2°47	14°50	18°20	S 21
M22	15 57 28	0♊40'33	28°12	7°38	15°26	0°46	1°12	6°38	19°38	27°16	0°16	3°50	2°44	14°57	18°23	M22
T 23	16 1 24	1°38'17	10♋33	8°10	16°28	1°21	1°25	6°40	19°42	27°17	0°16	3°45	2°41	15° 4	18°26	T 23
W24	16 5 21	2°35'59	22°42	8°47	17°31	1°55	1°39	6°43	19°45	27°18	0°15	3°41	2°38	15°10	18°29	W24
T 25	16 9 17	3°33'40	4♌42	9°27	18°32	2°29	1°52	6°45	19°49	27°19	0°14	3°37	2°35	15°17	18°31	T 25
F 26	16 13 14	4°31'20	16°36	10°11	19°34	3° 4	2° 5	6°47	19°52	27°21	0°14	3°34	2°32	15°24	18°34	F 26
S 27	16 17 10	5°28'57	28°28	10°59	20°35	3°38	2°18	6°49	19°55	27°22	0°13	3°33	2°28	15°31	18°37	S 27
S 28	16 21 7	6°26'34	10♍24	11°50	21°35	4°13	2°32	6°52	19°59	27°23	0°12	3°D33	2°25	15°37	18°39	S 28
M29	16 25 4	7°24'09	22°27	12°45	22°36	4°48	2°45	6°53	20° 2	27°24	0°12	3°33	2°22	15°44	18°42	M29
T 30	16 29 0	8°21'42	4♎42	13°43	23°36	5°22	2°58	6°55	20° 5	27°25	0°11	3°35	2°19	15°51	18°44	T 30
W31	16 32 57	9♊19'15	17♎15	14♉45	24♋35	5♌57	3♉11	6♓57	20♉ 9	27♓26	0♒10	3♉37	2♉16	15♌58	18♈47	W31

June 2023
Ephemeris

JUNE 2023 **00:00 UT**

Day	Sid.t	☉	☽	☿	♀	♂	♃	♄	♅	♆	♇	☊	☊	⚸	⚷	Day
T 1	16 36 53	10♊16'45	0♏ 8	15♉49	25♋35	6♌32	3♉24	6♓59	20♉12	27♓27	0°R 9	3°R37	2♉12	16♌ 4	18♈49	T 1
F 2	16 40 50	11°14'15	13°24	16°57	26°33	7° 7	3°37	7° 0	20°15	27°28	0♒ 9	3♉37	2° 9	16°11	18°52	F 2
S 3	16 44 46	12°11'44	27° 4	18° 8	27°32	7°41	3°49	7° 2	20°19	27°29	0° 8	3°35	2° 6	16°18	18°54	S 3
S 4	16 48 43	13° 9'11	11♐ 7	19°21	28°30	8°16	4° 2	7° 3	20°22	27°30	0° 7	3°31	2° 3	16°24	18°57	S 4
M 5	16 52 39	14° 6'38	25°27	20°38	29°27	8°51	4°15	7° 5	20°25	27°30	0° 6	3°26	2° 0	16°31	18°59	M 5
T 6	16 56 36	15° 4'03	10♑ 1	21°58	0♌24	9°26	4°27	7° 6	20°28	27°31	0° 5	3°20	1°57	16°38	19° 1	T 6
W 7	17 0 33	16° 1'28	24°41	23°20	1°21	10° 1	4°40	7° 7	20°32	27°32	0° 4	3°14	1°53	16°45	19° 4	W 7
T 8	17 4 29	16°58'52	9♒20	24°46	2°17	10°36	4°53	7° 8	20°35	27°33	0° 3	3° 8	1°50	16°51	19° 6	T 8
F 9	17 8 26	17°56'16	23°52	26°14	3°13	11°12	5° 5	7° 9	20°38	27°33	0° 2	3° 4	1°47	16°58	19° 8	F 9
S 10	17 12 22	18°53'38	8♓12	27°45	4° 8	11°47	5°17	7°10	20°41	27°34	0° 1	3° 2	1°44	17° 5	19°10	S 10
S 11	17 16 19	19°51'01	22°17	29°18	5° 2	12°22	5°30	7°10	20°44	27°35	0° 0	3°D 2	1°41	17°11	19°12	S 11
M12	17 20 15	20°48'22	6♈ 7	0♊55	5°56	12°57	5°42	7°11	20°47	27°35	29♑59	3° 2	1°38	17°18	19°14	M12
T 13	17 24 12	21°45'44	19°41	2°34	6°50	13°33	5°54	7°12	20°51	27°36	29°58	3° 3	1°34	17°25	19°16	T 13
W14	17 28 8	22°43'05	3♉ 2	4°16	7°43	14° 8	6° 6	7°12	20°54	27°37	29°57	3°R 4	1°31	17°32	19°18	W14
T 15	17 32 5	23°40'25	16° 9	6° 1	8°35	14°43	6°18	7°12	20°57	27°37	29°56	3° 3	1°28	17°38	19°20	T 15
F 16	17 36 2	24°37'45	29° 4	7°48	9°26	15°19	6°30	7°12	21° 0	27°38	29°55	3° 0	1°25	17°45	19°22	F 16
S 17	17 39 58	25°35'05	11♊47	9°38	10°17	15°54	6°41	7°13	21° 3	27°38	29°54	2°55	1°22	17°52	19°24	S 17
S 18	17 43 55	26°32'24	24°20	11°30	11° 8	16°30	6°53	7°R13	21° 6	27°39	29°53	2°48	1°18	17°58	19°26	S 18
M19	17 47 51	27°29'42	6♋42	13°25	11°57	17° 5	7° 5	7°13	21° 9	27°39	29°52	2°38	1°15	18° 5	19°27	M19
T 20	17 51 48	28°27'00	18°54	15°22	12°46	17°41	7°16	7°12	21°12	27°39	29°51	2°28	1°12	18°12	19°29	T 20
W21	17 55 44	29°24'17	0♌58	17°22	13°34	18°17	7°28	7°12	21°15	27°40	29°49	2°18	1° 9	18°19	19°31	W21
T 22	17 59 41	0♋21'34	12°55	19°24	14°22	18°53	7°39	7°12	21°18	27°40	29°48	2° 8	1° 6	18°25	19°32	T 22
F 23	18 3 37	1°18'50	24°47	21°27	15° 8	19°28	7°50	7°11	21°20	27°40	29°47	2° 1	1° 3	18°32	19°34	F 23
S 24	18 7 34	2°16'05	6♍37	23°33	15°54	20° 4	8° 2	7°11	21°23	27°40	29°46	1°55	0°59	18°39	19°35	S 24
S 25	18 11 31	3°13'20	18°31	25°40	16°39	20°40	8°13	7°10	21°26	27°41	29°45	1°52	0°56	18°46	19°37	S 25
M26	18 15 27	4°10'34	0♎32	27°48	17°22	21°16	8°24	7° 9	21°29	27°41	29°43	1°D51	0°53	18°52	19°38	M26
T 27	18 19 24	5° 7'47	12°45	29°58	18° 5	21°52	8°34	7° 8	21°32	27°41	29°42	1°51	0°50	18°59	19°40	T 27
W28	18 23 20	6° 5'00	25°15	2♋ 8	18°47	22°28	8°45	7° 7	21°34	27°41	29°41	1°R52	0°47	19° 6	19°41	W28
T 29	18 27 17	7° 2'13	8♏ 8	4°19	19°28	23° 4	8°56	7° 6	21°37	27°41	29°40	1°52	0°44	19°12	19°42	T 29
F 30	18 31 13	7♋59'25	21♏27	6♋30	20♌ 8	23♌40	9♉ 6	7♓ 5	21♉40	27♓41	29♑38	1♉50	0♉40	19♌19	19♈43	F 30

July 2023 Ephemeris

JULY 2023 **00:00 UT**

Day	Sid.t	☉	☽	☿	♀	♂	♃	♄	♅	♆	♇	☊	☊	⚸	⚷	Day
S 1	18 35 10	8♋56'36	5♐14	8♋41	20♌47	24♌16	9♉17	7°R 4	21♉42	27°R41	29°R37	1°R46	0♉37	19♌26	19♈45	S 1
S 2	18 39 6	9°53'48	19°28	10°52	21°24	24°52	9°27	7♓ 3	21°45	27♓41	29♑36	1♉40	0°34	19°33	19°46	S 2
M 3	18 43 3	10°50'59	4♑ 6	13° 2	22° 0	25°28	9°38	7° 1	21°47	27°41	29°34	1°32	0°31	19°39	19°47	M 3
T 4	18 47 0	11°48'10	19° 1	15°11	22°36	26° 4	9°48	7° 0	21°50	27°41	29°33	1°22	0°28	19°46	19°48	T 4
W 5	18 50 56	12°45'21	4♒ 5	17°19	23° 9	26°41	9°58	6°58	21°52	27°41	29°32	1°12	0°24	19°53	19°49	W 5
T 6	18 54 53	13°42'32	19° 7	19°26	23°42	27°17	10° 8	6°56	21°55	27°41	29°30	1° 3	0°21	19°59	19°50	T 6
F 7	18 58 49	14°39'43	3♓58	21°32	24°13	27°53	10°17	6°55	21°57	27°41	29°29	0°56	0°18	20° 6	19°51	F 7
S 8	19 2 46	15°36'55	18°32	23°36	24°42	28°29	10°27	6°53	22° 0	27°40	29°28	0°51	0°15	20°13	19°51	S 8
S 9	19 6 42	16°34'06	2♈45	25°39	25°11	29° 6	10°37	6°51	22° 2	27°40	29°26	0°49	0°12	20°20	19°52	S 9
M10	19 10 39	17°31'18	16°34	27°40	25°37	29°42	10°46	6°49	22° 4	27°40	29°25	0°D48	0° 9	20°26	19°53	M10
T 11	19 14 36	18°28'31	0♉ 3	29°39	26° 2	0♍19	10°56	6°46	22° 7	27°40	29°23	0°R48	0° 5	20°33	19°54	T 11
W12	19 18 32	19°25'44	13°11	1♌37	26°25	0°55	11° 5	6°44	22° 9	27°39	29°22	0°48	0° 2	20°40	19°54	W12
T 13	19 22 29	20°22'58	26° 4	3°33	26°47	1°32	11°14	6°42	22°11	27°39	29°21	0°46	29♈59	20°46	19°55	T 13
F 14	19 26 25	21°20'12	8♊42	5°26	27° 7	2° 8	11°23	6°39	22°13	27°38	29°19	0°41	29°56	20°53	19°55	F 14
S 15	19 30 22	22°17'26	21°10	7°18	27°25	2°45	11°32	6°37	22°15	27°38	29°18	0°34	29°53	21° 0	19°56	S 15
S 16	19 34 18	23°14'41	3♋28	9° 8	27°41	3°22	11°40	6°34	22°17	27°38	29°16	0°24	29°50	21° 7	19°56	S 16
M17	19 38 15	24°11'57	15°37	10°57	27°55	3°58	11°49	6°32	22°19	27°37	29°15	0°11	29°46	21°13	19°57	M17
T 18	19 42 11	25° 9'13	27°40	12°43	28° 7	4°35	11°58	6°29	22°21	27°37	29°13	29♈58	29°43	21°20	19°57	T 18
W19	19 46 8	26° 6'29	9♌38	14°27	28°18	5°12	12° 6	6°26	22°23	27°36	29°12	29°44	29°40	21°27	19°57	W19
T 20	19 50 5	27° 3'45	21°31	16°10	28°26	5°49	12°14	6°23	22°25	27°35	29°11	29°31	29°37	21°33	19°57	T 20
F 21	19 54 1	28° 1'02	3♍21	17°51	28°31	6°26	12°22	6°20	22°27	27°35	29° 9	29°20	29°34	21°40	19°58	F 21
S 22	19 57 58	28°58'19	15°11	19°29	28°35	7° 3	12°30	6°17	22°29	27°34	29° 8	29°12	29°30	21°47	19°58	S 22
S 23	20 1 54	29°55'36	27° 4	21° 6	28°R36	7°40	12°38	6°14	22°31	27°33	29° 6	29° 7	29°27	21°54	19°58	S 23
M24	20 5 51	0♌52'54	9♎ 4	22°42	28°35	8°17	12°45	6°11	22°32	27°33	29° 5	29° 4	29°24	22° 0	19°R58	M24
T 25	20 9 47	1°50'12	21°15	24°15	28°32	8°54	12°53	6° 8	22°34	27°32	29° 4	29° 3	29°21	22° 7	19°58	T 25
W26	20 13 44	2°47'31	3♏43	25°46	28°26	9°31	13° 0	6° 4	22°36	27°31	29° 2	29° 3	29°18	22°14	19°58	W26
T 27	20 17 40	3°44'49	16°32	27°16	28°18	10° 8	13° 7	6° 1	22°37	27°30	29° 1	29° 3	29°15	22°20	19°57	T 27
F 28	20 21 37	4°42'09	29°47	28°43	28° 7	10°45	13°14	5°57	22°39	27°30	28°59	29° 1	29°11	22°27	19°57	F 28
S 29	20 25 34	5°39'28	13♐31	0♍ 9	27°54	11°22	13°21	5°54	22°41	27°29	28°58	28°57	29° 8	22°34	19°57	S 29
S 30	20 29 30	6°36'49	27°44	1°32	27°39	11°59	13°28	5°50	22°42	27°28	28°56	28°51	29° 5	22°41	19°57	S 30
M31	20 33 27	7♌34'10	12♑26	2♍54	27♌21	12♍37	13♉35	5♓46	22♉44	27♓27	28♑55	28♈42	29♈ 2	22♌47	19♈56	M31

August 2023
Ephemeris

AUGUST 2023 | 00:00 UT

Day	Sid.t	☉	☽	☿	♀	♂	♃	♄	♅	♆	♇	☊	☊	⚸	⚷	Day
T 1	20 37 23	8♌31'31	27♑29	4♍14	27°R 1	13♍14	13♉41	5°R43	22♉45	27°R26	28°R54	28°R32	28♈59	22♌54	19°R56	T 1
W 2	20 41 20	9°28'53	12♒45	5°31	26♌39	13°51	13°47	5♓39	22°46	27♓25	28♑52	28♈21	28°56	23° 1	19♈55	W 2
T 3	20 45 16	10°26'16	28° 2	6°47	26°15	14°29	13°53	5°35	22°48	27°24	28°51	28°12	28°52	23° 7	19°55	T 3
F 4	20 49 13	11°23'40	13♓10	8° 0	25°49	15° 6	13°59	5°31	22°49	27°23	28°49	28° 4	28°49	23°14	19°54	F 4
S 5	20 53 9	12°21'05	27°59	9°11	25°20	15°44	14° 5	5°27	22°50	27°22	28°48	27°59	28°46	23°21	19°54	S 5
S 6	20 57 6	13°18'31	12♈23	10°20	24°50	16°21	14°11	5°23	22°51	27°21	28°47	27°56	28°43	23°28	19°53	S 6
M 7	21 1 3	14°15'59	26°21	11°26	24°19	16°59	14°16	5°19	22°52	27°20	28°45	27°D55	28°40	23°34	19°52	M 7
T 8	21 4 59	15°13'28	9♉52	12°30	23°46	17°36	14°21	5°15	22°53	27°19	28°44	27°R55	28°36	23°41	19°52	T 8
W 9	21 8 56	16°10'58	23° 0	13°31	23°11	18°14	14°26	5°11	22°54	27°18	28°43	27°55	28°33	23°48	19°51	W 9
T 10	21 12 52	17° 8'29	5♊47	14°30	22°36	18°52	14°31	5° 7	22°55	27°17	28°41	27°54	28°30	23°54	19°50	T 10
F 11	21 16 49	18° 6'02	18°17	15°25	22° 0	19°29	14°36	5° 3	22°56	27°15	28°40	27°50	28°27	24° 1	19°49	F 11
S 12	21 20 45	19° 3'36	0♋35	16°18	21°23	20° 7	14°41	4°58	22°57	27°14	28°39	27°44	28°24	24° 8	19°48	S 12
S 13	21 24 42	20° 1'12	12°42	17° 8	20°46	20°45	14°45	4°54	22°58	27°13	28°37	27°35	28°21	24°14	19°47	S 13
M14	21 28 38	20°58'49	24°43	17°54	20° 8	21°23	14°49	4°50	22°59	27°12	28°36	27°24	28°17	24°21	19°46	M14
T 15	21 32 35	21°56'27	6♌39	18°37	19°31	22° 1	14°53	4°45	23° 0	27°10	28°35	27°12	28°14	24°28	19°45	T 15
W16	21 36 32	22°54'06	18°32	19°16	18°54	22°39	14°57	4°41	23° 0	27° 9	28°33	27° 0	28°11	24°35	19°44	W16
T 17	21 40 28	23°51'47	0♍23	19°51	18°18	23°17	15° 1	4°37	23° 1	27° 8	28°32	26°49	28° 8	24°41	19°42	T 17
F 18	21 44 25	24°49'29	12°13	20°22	17°43	23°55	15° 5	4°32	23° 1	27° 7	28°31	26°39	28° 5	24°48	19°41	F 18
S 19	21 48 21	25°47'12	24° 6	20°49	17° 8	24°33	15° 8	4°28	23° 2	27° 5	28°30	26°32	28° 2	24°55	19°40	S 19
S 20	21 52 18	26°44'56	6♎ 2	21°12	16°35	25°11	15°11	4°23	23° 2	27° 4	28°28	26°28	27°58	25° 1	19°39	S 20
M21	21 56 14	27°42'42	18° 6	21°29	16° 3	25°49	15°14	4°19	23° 3	27° 2	28°27	26°25	27°55	25° 8	19°37	M21
T 22	22 0 11	28°40'28	0♏19	21°42	15°33	26°27	15°17	4°14	23° 3	27° 1	28°26	26°D25	27°52	25°15	19°36	T 22
W23	22 4 7	29°38'16	12°48	21°49	15° 4	27° 5	15°19	4°10	23° 4	27° 0	28°25	26°26	27°49	25°22	19°34	W23
T 24	22 8 4	0♍36'05	25°35	21°R51	14°38	27°44	15°22	4° 5	23° 4	26°58	28°24	26°R27	27°46	25°28	19°33	T 24
F 25	22 12 1	1°33'55	8♐46	21°47	14°13	28°22	15°24	4° 1	23° 4	26°57	28°23	26°27	27°42	25°35	19°31	F 25
S 26	22 15 57	2°31'47	22°23	21°38	13°50	29° 0	15°26	3°56	23° 4	26°55	28°21	26°25	27°39	25°42	19°30	S 26
S 27	22 19 54	3°29'40	6♑28	21°22	13°30	29°39	15°28	3°52	23° 4	26°54	28°20	26°21	27°36	25°48	19°28	S 27
M28	22 23 50	4°27'34	21° 0	21° 0	13°12	0♎17	15°29	3°47	23° 4	26°52	28°19	26°15	27°33	25°55	19°26	M28
T 29	22 27 47	5°25'29	5♒56	20°33	12°56	0°56	15°31	3°43	23°R 5	26°51	28°18	26° 8	27°30	26° 2	19°24	T 29
W30	22 31 43	6°23'25	21° 7	20° 0	12°43	1°34	15°32	3°38	23° 4	26°49	28°17	26° 1	27°27	26° 9	19°23	W30
T 31	22 35 40	7♍21'23	6♓24	19♍21	12♌32	2♎13	15♉33	3♓34	23♉ 4	26♓48	28♑16	25♈54	27♈23	26♌15	19♈21	T 31

September 2023 Ephemeris

SEPTEMBER 2023 **00:00 UT**

Day	Sid.t	☉	☽	☿	♀	♂	♃	♄	♅	♆	♇	☊	☊	⚸	⚷	Day
F 1	22 39 36	8♍19'23	21♓36	18°R37	12°R23	2♎51	15♉34	3°R29	23°R 4	26°R46	28°R15	25°R48	27♈20	26♌22	19°R19	F 1
S 2	22 43 33	9°17'24	6♈33	17♍48	12♌17	3°30	15°34	3♓25	23♉ 4	26♓45	28♑14	25♈45	27°17	26°29	19♈17	S 2
S 3	22 47 30	10°15'27	21° 7	16°55	12°14	4° 9	15°35	3°20	23° 4	26°43	28°13	25°D43	27°14	26°35	19°15	S 3
M 4	22 51 26	11°13'32	5♉15	16° 0	12°D12	4°47	15°35	3°16	23° 4	26°42	28°12	25°44	27°11	26°42	19°13	M 4
T 5	22 55 23	12°11'39	18°54	15° 2	12°13	5°26	15°R35	3°11	23° 3	26°40	28°11	25°45	27° 7	26°49	19°11	T 5
W 6	22 59 19	13° 9'48	2♊ 7	14° 4	12°17	6° 5	15°35	3° 7	23° 3	26°38	28°10	25°46	27° 4	26°55	19° 9	W 6
T 7	23 3 16	14° 7'59	14°56	13° 6	12°22	6°44	15°34	3° 2	23° 3	26°37	28° 9	25°R47	27° 1	27° 2	19° 7	T 7
F 8	23 7 12	15° 6'12	27°26	12°10	12°30	7°23	15°34	2°58	23° 2	26°35	28° 8	25°46	26°58	27° 9	19° 5	F 8
S 9	23 11 9	16° 4'27	9♋41	11°16	12°40	8° 2	15°33	2°53	23° 2	26°34	28° 8	25°43	26°55	27°16	19° 3	S 9
S 10	23 15 5	17° 2'44	21°44	10°27	12°52	8°41	15°32	2°49	23° 1	26°32	28° 7	25°39	26°52	27°22	19° 1	S 10
M11	23 19 2	18° 1'03	3♌40	9°44	13° 7	9°20	15°31	2°45	23° 0	26°30	28° 6	25°33	26°48	27°29	18°58	M11
T 12	23 22 59	18°59'24	15°32	9° 7	13°23	9°59	15°29	2°40	23° 0	26°29	28° 5	25°27	26°45	27°36	18°56	T 12
W13	23 26 55	19°57'47	27°23	8°37	13°41	10°38	15°28	2°36	22°59	26°27	28° 4	25°20	26°42	27°42	18°54	W13
T 14	23 30 52	20°56'12	9♍15	8°16	14° 1	11°17	15°26	2°32	22°58	26°25	28° 4	25°14	26°39	27°49	18°51	T 14
F 15	23 34 48	21°54'39	21° 9	8° 4	14°23	11°56	15°24	2°28	22°57	26°24	28° 3	25° 8	26°36	27°56	18°49	F 15
S 16	23 38 45	22°53'07	3♎ 8	8°D 0	14°47	12°36	15°22	2°24	22°57	26°22	28° 2	25° 5	26°33	28° 2	18°47	S 16
S 17	23 42 41	23°51'38	15°13	8° 6	15°12	13°15	15°19	2°20	22°56	26°20	28° 2	25° 3	26°29	28° 9	18°44	S 17
M18	23 46 38	24°50'10	27°27	8°22	15°39	13°54	15°17	2°16	22°55	26°19	28° 1	25°D 2	26°26	28°16	18°42	M18
T 19	23 50 34	25°48'44	9♏51	8°47	16° 8	14°34	15°14	2°12	22°54	26°17	28° 0	25° 3	26°23	28°23	18°39	T 19
W20	23 54 31	26°47'20	22°28	9°21	16°38	15°13	15°11	2° 8	22°53	26°15	28° 0	25° 5	26°20	28°29	18°37	W20
T 21	23 58 28	27°45'57	5♐21	10° 4	17° 9	15°53	15° 8	2° 4	22°52	26°14	27°59	25° 6	26°17	28°36	18°35	T 21
F 22	0 2 24	28°44'36	18°33	10°55	17°42	16°32	15° 5	2° 0	22°50	26°12	27°59	25° 8	26°13	28°43	18°32	F 22
S 23	0 6 21	29°43'17	2♑ 5	11°54	18°16	17°12	15° 1	1°56	22°49	26°10	27°58	25°R 8	26°10	28°49	18°29	S 23
S 24	0 10 17	0♎42'00	16° 1	13° 0	18°52	17°52	14°57	1°53	22°48	26° 9	27°58	25° 7	26° 7	28°56	18°27	S 24
M25	0 14 14	1°40'44	0♒18	14°12	19°29	18°31	14°53	1°49	22°47	26° 7	27°57	25° 5	26° 4	29° 3	18°24	M25
T 26	0 18 10	2°39'30	14°56	15°31	20° 7	19°11	14°49	1°45	22°45	26° 6	27°57	25° 3	26° 1	29° 9	18°22	T 26
W27	0 22 7	3°38'18	29°49	16°54	20°46	19°51	14°45	1°42	22°44	26° 4	27°56	25° 0	25°58	29°16	18°19	W27
T 28	0 26 3	4°37'07	14♓49	18°22	21°27	20°31	14°40	1°38	22°43	26° 2	27°56	24°57	25°54	29°23	18°17	T 28
F 29	0 30 0	5°35'58	29°49	19°54	22° 9	21°10	14°36	1°35	22°41	26° 1	27°56	24°55	25°51	29°30	18°14	F 29
S 30	0 33 56	6♎34'51	14♈40	21♍30	22♌51	21♎50	14♉31	1♓32	22♉40	25♓59	27♑55	24♈54	25♈48	29♌36	18♈11	S 30

October 2023 Ephemeris

OCTOBER 2023 **00:00 UT**

Day	Sid.t	☉	☽	☿	♀	♂	♃	♄	♅	♆	♇	☊	Ω	⚸	⚷	Day
S 1	0 37 53	7♎33'47	29♈13	23♍ 8	23♌35	22♎30	14°R26	1°R29	22°R38	25°R57	27°R55	24°D54	25♈45	29♌43	18°R 9	S 1
M 2	0 41 50	8°32'44	13♉24	24°48	24°20	23°10	14♉21	1♓25	22♉37	25♓56	27♑55	24♈54	25°42	29°50	18♈ 6	M 2
T 3	0 45 46	9°31'44	27°10	26°31	25° 5	23°50	14°16	1°22	22°35	25°54	27°54	24°55	25°39	29°56	18° 3	T 3
W 4	0 49 43	10°30'46	10♊29	28°15	25°52	24°30	14°10	1°19	22°34	25°53	27°54	24°57	25°35	0♍ 3	18° 1	W 4
T 5	0 53 39	11°29'50	23°24	29°59	26°39	25°11	14° 4	1°16	22°32	25°51	27°54	24°58	25°32	0°10	17°58	T 5
F 6	0 57 36	12°28'57	5♋58	1♎45	27°28	25°51	13°59	1°14	22°30	25°49	27°54	24°58	25°29	0°16	17°55	F 6
S 7	1 1 32	13°28'06	18°14	3°31	28°17	26°31	13°53	1°11	22°28	25°48	27°54	24°R58	25°26	0°23	17°52	S 7
S 8	1 5 29	14°27'17	0♌18	5°17	29° 7	27°11	13°47	1° 8	22°27	25°46	27°54	24°58	25°23	0°30	17°50	S 8
M 9	1 9 26	15°26'31	12°13	7° 4	29°57	27°52	13°40	1° 5	22°25	25°45	27°54	24°57	25°19	0°37	17°47	M 9
T 10	1 13 22	16°25'46	24° 4	8°50	0♍49	28°32	13°34	1° 3	22°23	25°43	27°54	24°56	25°16	0°43	17°44	T 10
W11	1 17 19	17°25'04	5♍55	10°36	1°41	29°13	13°28	1° 1	22°21	25°42	27°D54	24°55	25°13	0°50	17°41	W11
T 12	1 21 15	18°24'24	17°49	12°22	2°34	29°53	13°21	0°58	22°19	25°40	27°54	24°54	25°10	0°57	17°39	T 12
F 13	1 25 12	19°23'47	29°49	14° 8	3°28	0♏34	13°14	0°56	22°17	25°39	27°54	24°53	25° 7	1° 3	17°36	F 13
S 14	1 29 8	20°23'11	11♎57	15°53	4°22	1°14	13° 7	0°54	22°15	25°37	27°54	24°53	25° 4	1°10	17°33	S 14
S 15	1 33 5	21°22'38	24°16	17°37	5°17	1°55	13° 0	0°52	22°13	25°36	27°54	24°D52	25° 0	1°17	17°31	S 15
M16	1 37 1	22°22'06	6♏46	19°21	6°12	2°36	12°53	0°50	22°11	25°34	27°54	24°53	24°57	1°23	17°28	M16
T 17	1 40 58	23°21'37	19°28	21° 4	7° 8	3°16	12°46	0°48	22° 9	25°33	27°54	24°53	24°54	1°30	17°25	T 17
W18	1 44 54	24°21'10	2♐23	22°47	8° 4	3°57	12°39	0°46	22° 7	25°31	27°54	24°53	24°51	1°37	17°22	W18
T 19	1 48 51	25°20'44	15°32	24°29	9° 1	4°38	12°31	0°44	22° 5	25°30	27°54	24°R53	24°48	1°44	17°20	T 19
F 20	1 52 48	26°20'20	28°55	26°11	9°59	5°19	12°24	0°43	22° 3	25°29	27°55	24°53	24°45	1°50	17°17	F 20
S 21	1 56 44	27°19'58	12♑33	27°51	10°57	6° 0	12°16	0°41	22° 1	25°27	27°55	24°53	24°41	1°57	17°14	S 21
S 22	2 0 41	28°19'38	26°26	29°32	11°56	6°41	12° 8	0°40	21°58	25°26	27°55	24°D52	24°38	2° 4	17°12	S 22
M23	2 4 37	29°19'20	10♒33	1♏11	12°55	7°22	12° 1	0°39	21°56	25°25	27°56	24°53	24°35	2°10	17° 9	M23
T 24	2 8 34	0♏19'03	24°52	2°50	13°54	8° 3	11°53	0°37	21°54	25°23	27°56	24°53	24°32	2°17	17° 6	T 24
W25	2 12 30	1°18'47	9♓20	4°29	14°54	8°44	11°45	0°36	21°52	25°22	27°56	24°53	24°29	2°24	17° 4	W25
T 26	2 16 27	2°18'34	23°54	6° 6	15°55	9°25	11°37	0°35	21°49	25°21	27°57	24°54	24°25	2°30	17° 1	T 26
F 27	2 20 23	3°18'22	8♈29	7°44	16°55	10° 7	11°29	0°34	21°47	25°20	27°57	24°55	24°22	2°37	16°59	F 27
S 28	2 24 20	4°18'12	22°59	9°20	17°57	10°48	11°21	0°34	21°45	25°18	27°58	24°R55	24°19	2°44	16°56	S 28
S 29	2 28 17	5°18'03	7♉17	10°57	18°58	11°29	11°13	0°33	21°42	25°17	27°58	24°55	24°16	2°50	16°53	S 29
M30	2 32 13	6°17'57	21°19	12°32	20° 0	12°11	11° 5	0°32	21°40	25°16	27°59	24°54	24°13	2°57	16°51	M30
T 31	2 36 10	7♏17'53	5♊ 1	14♏ 8	21♍ 3	12♏52	10♉57	0♓32	21♉38	25♓15	27♑59	24♈52	24♈10	3♍ 4	16♈48	T 31

November 2023 Ephemeris

00:00 UT

Day	Sid.t	☉	☽	☿	♀	♂	♃	♄	♅	♆	♇	☊	⚷	⚸
W 1	2 40 6	8♏17 51	18Ⅱ22	15♏42	22♍ 5	13♏34	10°R49	0°R31	21°R35	25°R14	28♑ 0	24♈R51	24♈ 6	3♍11	16°R46
T 2	2 44 3	9°17 51	15♋20	17°17	23° 9	14°15	10°40	0°31	21°33	25°13	28° 1	24♈49	24° 3	3°17	16♈43
F 3	2 47 59	10°17 53	13°57	18°50	24°12	14°57	10°32	0°31	21°30	25°12	28° 1	24°47	24° 0	3°24	16°41
S 4	2 51 56	11°17 58	26°17	20°24	25°16	15°38	10°24	0°D31	21°28	25°11	28° 2	24°45	23°57	3°31	16°38
S 5	2 55 52	12°18 04	8♌22	21°57	26°20	16°20	10°16	0°31	21°25	25°10	28° 3	24°D45	23°54	3°37	16°36
M 6	2 59 49	13°18 12	20°18	23°29	27°24	17° 2	10° 8	0°31	21°23	25° 9	28° 3	24°45	23°50	3°44	16°34
T 7	3 3 46	14°18 23	2♍ 9	25° 1	28°29	17°44	10° 0	0°31	21°20	25° 8	28° 4	24°46	23°47	3°51	16°31
W 8	3 7 42	15°18 35	14° 0	26°33	29°34	18°25	9°52	0°32	21°18	25° 7	28° 5	24°47	23°44	3°57	16°29
T 9	3 11 39	16°18 50	25°56	28° 5	0♎39	19° 7	9°43	0°32	21°16	25° 6	28° 6	24°49	23°41	4° 4	16°27
F 10	3 15 35	17°19 06	8♎ 0	29°36	1°45	19°49	9°35	0°33	21°13	25° 5	28° 7	24°50	23°38	4°11	16°24
S 11	3 19 32	18°19 24	20°17	1♏ 6	2°51	20°31	9°27	0°33	21°11	25° 4	28° 7	24°R51	23°35	4°17	16°22
S 12	3 23 28	19°19 44	2♏49	2°37	3°57	21°13	9°20	0°34	21° 8	25° 3	28° 8	24°51	23°31	4°24	16°20
M 13	3 27 25	20°20 06	15°37	4° 7	5° 3	21°55	9°12	0°35	21° 6	25° 3	28° 9	24°50	23°28	4°31	16°18
T 14	3 31 21	21°20 30	28°41	5°36	6°10	22°38	9° 4	0°36	21° 3	25° 2	28°10	24°47	23°25	4°38	16°16
W 15	3 35 18	22°20 56	12♐ 2	7° 5	7°17	23°20	8°56	0°37	21° 1	25° 1	28°11	24°43	23°22	4°44	16°14
T 16	3 39 15	23°21 23	25°36	8°34	8°24	24° 2	8°48	0°38	20°58	25° 0	28°12	24°38	23°19	4°51	16°12
F 17	3 43 11	24°21 51	9♑23	10° 2	9°31	24°44	8°41	0°39	20°56	25° 0	28°13	24°34	23°16	4°58	16°10
S 18	3 47 8	25°22 21	23°19	11°30	10°39	25°27	8°33	0°41	20°53	24°59	28°14	24°30	23°12	5° 4	16° 8
S 19	3 51 4	26°22 52	7♒21	12°58	11°47	26° 9	8°26	0°42	20°51	24°58	28°15	24°27	23° 9	5°11	16° 6
M 20	3 55 1	27°23 25	21°28	14°24	12°55	26°51	8°19	0°44	20°48	24°58	28°16	24°D26	23° 6	5°18	16° 4
T 21	3 58 57	28°23 58	5♓37	15°50	14° 3	27°34	8°11	0°45	20°46	24°57	28°18	24°26	23° 3	5°24	16° 2
W 22	4 2 54	29°24 33	19°47	17°16	15°11	28°17	8° 4	0°47	20°43	24°57	28°19	24°27	23° 0	5°31	16° 0
T 23	4 6 50	0♐25 08	3♈56	18°41	16°20	28°59	7°57	0°49	20°41	24°56	28°20	24°28	22°56	5°38	15°58
F 24	4 10 47	1°25 45	18° 2	20° 5	17°28	29°42	7°51	0°51	20°38	24°56	28°21	24°R29	22°53	5°44	15°57
S 25	4 14 44	2°26 23	2♉ 3	21°28	18°37	0♐24	7°44	0°53	20°36	24°56	28°22	24°29	22°50	5°51	15°55
S 26	4 18 40	3°27 03	15°56	22°49	19°46	1° 7	7°37	0°55	20°33	24°55	28°24	24°27	22°47	5°58	15°53
M 27	4 22 37	4°27 43	29°37	24°10	20°55	1°50	7°31	0°58	20°31	24°55	28°25	24°23	22°44	6° 4	15°52
T 28	4 26 33	5°28 26	13Ⅱ 5	25°29	22° 5	2°33	7°24	1° 0	20°29	24°55	28°26	24°18	22°41	6°11	15°50
W 29	4 30 30	6°29 09	26°16	26°47	23°14	3°16	7°18	1° 2	20°26	24°54	28°28	24°10	22°37	6°18	15°49
T 30	4 34 26	7♐29 54	9♋ 9	28♐ 3	24♎24	3♐59	7♏12	1♓ 5	20♉24	24♓54	28♑29	24♈ 2	22♈34	6♍25	15♈47

December 2023
Ephemeris

DECEMBER 2023 **00:00 UT**

Day	Sid.t	☉	☽	☿	♀	♂	♃	♄	♅	♆	♇	☊	☊	⚸	⚷	Day
F 1	4 38 23	8♐30'40	21♋45	29♐17	25♎34	4♐42	7°R 6	1♓ 8	20°R22	24°R54	28♑30	23°R55	22♈31	6♍31	15°R46	F 1
S 2	4 42 20	9°31'28	4♌ 5	0♑28	26°44	5°25	7♉ 1	1°11	20♉19	24♓54	28°32	23♈48	22°28	6°38	15♈44	S 2
S 3	4 46 16	10°32'17	16°10	1°36	27°54	6° 8	6°55	1°13	20°17	24°54	28°33	23°43	22°25	6°45	15°43	S 3
M 4	4 50 13	11°33'07	28° 6	2°42	29° 5	6°51	6°50	1°16	20°15	24°53	28°34	23°39	22°22	6°51	15°42	M 4
T 5	4 54 9	12°33'59	9♍57	3°44	0♏15	7°34	6°44	1°19	20°12	24°53	28°36	23°D38	22°18	6°58	15°41	T 5
W 6	4 58 6	13°34'52	21°47	4°41	1°26	8°17	6°39	1°23	20°10	24°53	28°37	23°38	22°15	7° 5	15°39	W 6
T 7	5 2 2	14°35'46	3♎42	5°34	2°36	9° 1	6°34	1°26	20° 8	24°D53	28°39	23°40	22°12	7°11	15°38	T 7
F 8	5 5 59	15°36'41	15°48	6°21	3°47	9°44	6°30	1°29	20° 6	24°53	28°40	23°41	22° 9	7°18	15°37	F 8
S 9	5 9 55	16°37'38	28° 8	7° 2	4°58	10°27	6°25	1°33	20° 4	24°53	28°42	23°R41	22° 6	7°25	15°36	S 9
S 10	5 13 52	17°38'36	10♏47	7°37	6° 9	11°11	6°21	1°36	20° 1	24°54	28°43	23°39	22° 2	7°31	15°35	S 10
M11	5 17 49	18°39'35	23°48	8° 3	7°21	11°54	6°17	1°40	19°59	24°54	28°45	23°35	21°59	7°38	15°34	M11
T 12	5 21 45	19°40'36	7♐12	8°21	8°32	12°38	6°13	1°43	19°57	24°54	28°47	23°29	21°56	7°45	15°33	T 12
W13	5 25 42	20°41'37	20°57	8°R29	9°43	13°21	6° 9	1°47	19°55	24°54	28°48	23°20	21°53	7°51	15°33	W13
T 14	5 29 38	21°42'39	4♑59	8°27	10°55	14° 5	6° 5	1°51	19°53	24°54	28°50	23°10	21°50	7°58	15°32	T 14
F 15	5 33 35	22°43'42	19°15	8°14	12° 7	14°49	6° 2	1°55	19°51	24°55	28°51	23° 0	21°47	8° 5	15°31	F 15
S 16	5 37 31	23°44'45	3♒39	7°49	13°18	15°33	5°59	1°59	19°49	24°55	28°53	22°51	21°43	8°11	15°31	S 16
S 17	5 41 28	24°45'49	18° 3	7°13	14°30	16°16	5°56	2° 3	19°47	24°55	28°55	22°44	21°40	8°18	15°30	S 17
M18	5 45 24	25°46'53	2♓24	6°25	15°42	17° 0	5°53	2° 7	19°45	24°56	28°56	22°39	21°37	8°25	15°29	M18
T 19	5 49 21	26°47'57	16°38	5°27	16°54	17°44	5°50	2°12	19°44	24°56	28°58	22°37	21°34	8°32	15°29	T 19
W20	5 53 18	27°49'02	0♈43	4°19	18° 6	18°28	5°48	2°16	19°42	24°56	29° 0	22°D36	21°31	8°38	15°29	W20
T 21	5 57 14	28°50'07	14°38	3° 4	19°18	19°12	5°45	2°21	19°40	24°57	29° 2	22°37	21°28	8°45	15°28	T 21
F 22	6 1 11	29°51'12	28°23	1°44	20°30	19°56	5°43	2°25	19°38	24°57	29° 3	22°R37	21°24	8°52	15°28	F 22
S 23	6 5 7	0♑52'18	11♉59	0°22	21°43	20°40	5°42	2°30	19°37	24°58	29° 5	22°35	21°21	8°58	15°28	S 23
S 24	6 9 4	1°53'24	25°25	28♐59	22°55	21°24	5°40	2°34	19°35	24°59	29° 7	22°31	21°18	9° 5	15°27	S 24
M25	6 13 0	2°54'30	8♊42	27°40	24° 8	22° 8	5°39	2°39	19°33	24°59	29° 9	22°24	21°15	9°12	15°27	M25
T 26	6 16 57	3°55'36	21°47	26°27	25°20	22°52	5°38	2°44	19°32	25° 0	29°10	22°14	21°12	9°18	15°27	T 26
W27	6 20 53	4°56'43	4♋40	25°20	26°33	23°37	5°37	2°49	19°30	25° 1	29°12	22° 2	21° 8	9°25	15°D27	W27
T 28	6 24 50	5°57'50	17°21	24°23	27°45	24°21	5°36	2°54	19°29	25° 1	29°14	21°48	21° 5	9°32	15°27	T 28
F 29	6 28 47	6°58'57	29°48	23°36	28°58	25° 5	5°35	2°59	19°27	25° 2	29°16	21°35	21° 2	9°38	15°27	F 29
S 30	6 32 43	8° 0'04	12♌ 2	22°59	0♐11	25°50	5°35	3° 4	19°26	25° 3	29°18	21°22	20°59	9°45	15°27	S 30
S 31	6 36 40	9♑ 1'12	24♌ 5	22♐33	1♐24	26♐34	5°D35	3♓ 9	19♉24	25♓ 4	29♑20	21♈12	20♈56	9♍52	15♈28	S 31

About the Authors

Drs. Ralph & Lahni DeAmicis have been professional Astrologers since the early 1970's. They met at Princeton University at the landmark Project Hindsight Research Conference in 1994. This had a profound influence on their professional work. In 2002 they became the Calendar's new Astrologers, and they added a forecast that explored the ongoing Transits. They chose this format over a generic Sun Sign column, and it has turned out to be a popular and helpful planning tool. In 2019 their company, Cuore Libre Publishing, took over the calendar. They spend their time consulting on Feng Shui and Astrology, improving the calendar and their books and developing TV shows, which can be found at www.SpaceAndTime.com.

Space and Time Publishing Catalog

Planetary Calendar Astrology, Moving Beyond Observation Into Action. Designed as a companion to the Calendar, it includes an entertaining introduction to Astrological principles and various powerful Location and Healing techniques that the authors use in their practice and forecasts. $22.00.

Feng Shui and the Tango, The Dance of Design
Do you want more fun, romance, commitment, acclaim and improved cash flow? The book shows you how to program your surroundings for attaining what you wan. 288 pages, $17.99. The 'Tango' Series includes Prosperity Lessons &Happiness Lessons.

The Dream Desk Quiz, Improving Personal & Team Performance Through Recognizing Your Ergo Dynamic Personality. Seven multiple choice questions and forty-three personalized answers to help unleash your talents, leadership skills and team cooperation. 92 pages, $9.95.

The 10 Minute Herbalist Series, This collection of short chapters gets right to the point with solutions that help resolve many of today's most persistent health problems, based on forty years plus of practical experience. 148 pages, $12.95. This series includes A Year of Healthful Hints, Ideas for Living a Healthy Life! & Good Health is Easy, It's Being Sick That's Rough!

Quick Reference: Timing

Taking Advantage of the Planetary Energies

When Planets are above the Dotted Line actions are supported. Delay these actions when the Planets are below the Dotted Line.

☉ **SUN:** Time to ask favors from superiors, to have dealings with attorneys or government. Start publicity.

☽ **MOON:** Time to handle the public, straighten affairs at home and deal with women. Watch the four quarters of the moon for planting.

☿ **MERCURY:** Start writing, start publishing, start intellectual pursuits, study, learn. Deliver public addresses.

♀ **VENUS:** Commence romance, start to gain favor of the opposite sex. Buy jewelry, clothes. Participate in art, music or entertainment.

♂ **MARS:** Start work on machinery, undergo surgery, start construction, organize sales force. Advance business.

♃ **JUPITER:** Take care of money matters, sign contracts. Start or search for new business. Time to start speculating.

♄ **SATURN:** Start building projects, handle real estate deals, develop mining. Start repairing, plumbing and digging.

♅ **URANUS:** Begin experiments, inventions and new ideas. Start traveling, especially by air. Investigate important propositions.

♆ **NEPTUNE:** Start water trips, start brewing, mix strange chemicals. Start poetry, shipping, investigate secrets.

♇ **PLUTO:** Start organizations, foundations and new principles. Time to "turn over a new leaf."

Quick Reference: 2023 Planetary Retrogrades

MERCURY..Dec. 29, 2022, 1:31am 24°♑ ..... Jan. 18, 5:11am 8°♑
April 21, 1:34am 15°♉ .... May 14, 8:16pm 5°♉
Aug 23, 12:59pm 21°♍ .... Sep 15, 1:20pm 8°♍
Dec 12, 11:08pm 8°♑ .... Jan 1, 2024 7:07pm 22° ♐
VENUS....... July 22, 6:32pm 28°♌ .... Sep 3, 6:19pm 12°♌
MARS........ Oct 30, 2022, 6:25am 25°♊........Jan 12, 12:56pm 8°♊
JUPITER.... Sep 4, 7:10am 15°♉..................... Dec 30, 6:40pm 5°♉
SATURN.... Jun 17, 10:27am 7°♓ .... Nov 4, 12:02am 0°♓
URANUS.... Aug 24, 2022 6:52am 18°♉ ...... Jan 22, 2:58pm 14°♉
Aug 28, 7:38pm 23°♉.... Jan 26, 2024, 11:34pm 19°♉
NEPTUNE.. Jun 30, 2:06pm 27°♓................... Dec 6, 5:21am 24°♓
PLUTO....... May 1, 10:08am 0°♒ .... Oct 10, 6:09pm 27°♑

2023 Eclipses

Apr 30, 1:28pm - Partial Solar 10°♉ | May 15, 9:14pm - Total Lunar 25°♏
Oct 25, 3:48am - Partial Solar 2°♏ | Nov 8, 3:02am - Total Lunar 16°♉

Gardening

These recommendations come from Biodynamic Farming, the oldest modern organic farming method, established after WWI, which uses an Astrological Gardening Calendar to time all of its actions.
On Water Moon Days plant and tend to leaf plants like lettuce, spinach, celery and cabbage. ♋ Cancer, ♏ Scorpio, ♓ Pisces.
On Fire Moon Days plant, tend and harvest fruits, nuts, seeds and gourds like cherries, pumpkins, oranges. ♈Aries, ♌ Leo, ♐ Sagittarius. **On Earth Moon Days** plant and tend root crops like yams, carrots, radishes. It is a good day to store crops. ♉ Taurus, ♍ Virgo, ♑ Capricorn. **On Air Moon Days** plant and tend flowering plants and harvest medicinal herbs like mints and basil, ♊ Gemini, ♎ Libra, ♒ Aquarius.

The New Moon is a time for rest, celebration and meditation.
The Full Moon is a time for rest, celebration and meditation as well as a good time to harvest all crops, especially medicinal plants.

Ordering Next Year's Planetary Calendars & Day Planners

Calendars are ready in the Summer of the current year. Advance orders are mailed as soon as the Calendars are available when prepaid with a check, money order or credit card. Please include your contact info in case there are questions about your order. **FOR INTERNATIONAL ORDERS** please email us before ordering for a shipping quote at Sales@SpaceAndTime.com

In the USA: XL Wall $20.00 – Original Wall $18.00 Mini Pocket $15.00 – Day Planner $22.00 Digital for Cell Phones & Tablets $15.00

U.S. Funds Only - price includes USA shipping

ORDER ONLINE at www.PlanetaryCalendar.com

MAIL ORDERS TO:
Planetary Calendar
PO Box 5391 Napa, CA 94581-0391

PHONE ORDERS or CUSTOMER SERVICE
Please leave a Voicemail w/your Email at **(800) 217-4197**

We accept AmEx, Disc, MC and Visa via Phone & Online. Credit card orders require full name, billing address, phone number & email along with credit card #, exp date, & security code. Except for pre-orders, we ship weekly but please allow 4-6 weeks for delivery because we are not responsible for postal delays.

Planetary Calendar Since 1949

www.ingramcontent.com/pod-product-compliance
Lightning Source LLC
Chambersburg PA
CBHW050316120526
44592CB00014B/1926